access to philosophy

SEX AND
RELATIONSHIPS

Michael Wilcockson

Hodder & Stoughton
A MEMBER OF THE HODDER HEADLINE GROUP

Acknowledgements

The publisher would like to thank the following for permission to reproduce copyright illustrations in this book: cover illustration, Pablo Picasso. The Lovers, 1923 copyright Succession Picasso/DACS 2000/(National Gallery of Art, Washington DC) The Bridgeman Art Library, London. Page 154, Popperfoto.

The publishers would also like to thank the following for permission to reproduce the material in this book:

Cambridge University Press for the extract from *Feminism and Christian Ethics* by S Parsons, 1996; Jonathan Cape for the extract from *The Second Sex* by Simone de Beauvoir; Continuum International Publishing Group Ltd. for the extract from *Catechism of The Catholic Church* by 1994; Epworth Press for an extract from *Groundwork of Christian Ethics* by R Jones,1984; Gillon Aitken Associates Ltd. for the extract from *Sex and Destiny* by Germaine Greer, 1984; Inter-Varsity Press for the extracts from *Straight and Narrow* by T Schmidt, 1995; Penguin UK for the extracts from *On Liberty* by J S Mill, 1974, and an extract from *The Use of Pleasure: The History of Sexuality* vol. 1 by Michael Foucault, 1984; Sage Publications for extracts from *The New Family* by E Silva and C Smart; SCM Press for extracts from *After Christianity* by Daphne Hampson, 1996; we are grateful to Mr John Wolters for permission to reproduce the extract on p37 from the Clifton Wolters translation of Julian of Norwich, *Revelations of Divine Love*.

Every effort has been made to trace and acknowledge ownership of copyright. The publishers will be glad to make arrangements with any copyright holders with whom it has not been possible to contact.

Orders: please contact Bookpoint Ltd, 130 Milton Park, Abingdon, Oxon OX14 4SB. Telephone: (44) 01235 827720, Fax: (44) 01235 400454. Lines are open from 9.00–6.00, Monday to Saturday, with a 24 hour message answer service. Email address: orders@bookpoint.co.uk

British Library Cataloguing in Publication Data
A catalogue for this title is available from the British Library

ISBN 0 340 72489 7

First published 2000

Impression number	10	9	8	7	6	5	4	3	2
Year			2006	2005	2004	2003	2002	2001	

Typeset by Transet Limited, Coventry, England.
Printed in Great Britain for Hodder & Stoughton Educational, a division of Hodder Headline Plc, 338 Euston Road, London NW1 3BH by The Bath Press, Bath

Contents

Preface

To the general reader

Although *Access* books have been designed mainly to meet the needs of examination students, they also have much to offer the general reader. *Access* authors are committed to writing up-to-date scholarly texts in an easily accessible format. The main body of the text should therefore provide a readable and engaging survey of the subject, in easily digestible sections. Clarity is further enhanced by sub-headings and bullet-points.

To the student reader

Access books are written mainly for students studying for examinations at higher level, particularly GCE Advanced Subsidiary (AS) Level and Advanced (A2) Level and Scottish Highers. A number of features have been included to assist students, such as the word-lists at the beginning of chapters and the material at the end of chapters.

To use this book most effectively, you should be aware of the following features.

- The introductory chapter will set the scene for the material in the rest of the book.
- The Contents gives a break-down of the sections in each chapter.
- If you turn to the relevant chapters, you will find that they are broken down further into sub-headings and bullet-points. There are sometimes also Key Issues to focus your attention on important points.
- The Key Words at the beginning of each chapter are for easy reference and to help you become more familiar with the technical language of the subject.
- At the end of each chapter is a Summary of the main points, presented either as lists or diagrams. This is a useful quick revision tool. The list can also form the outline of your own notes on the topic.
- There may be some suggestions for further reading on the topic.
- There is also a range of typical examination questions, with some specific advice on how to answer them. Do tackle the specimen questions, planning your answers to some of them and writing some in full.

General advice on answering essay questions
Structured questions will tell you what to include. The following advice is for those questions which leave it to you to work out.

- The most important thing is to read the question carefully and work out what it really means. Make sure you understand all the words in the question (you may need to check some of them in the dictionary or look up technical terms in the Word Lists in the book).

● Gather the relevant information for answering the question. You will probably *not* need everything you know on the topic. Keep to what the question is asking.

● Organise your material by drawing up a plan of paragraphs. Make sure that each paragraph is relevant to the question. Include different views within your answer (most questions require arguments for and against).

● Start with an introduction which explains in your own words what the question is asking and defines any technical words. Work through your answer in your carefully planned paragraphs. Write a brief conclusion in which you sum up your answer to the question (without repeating everything in the essay).

1 Introduction

It is sometimes said that men think about sex once every four or five seconds. Whether this is literally true or not it serves to illustrate that human sexuality is at the very heart of being human. The title of this book is 'Sex and relationships' because 'sex' is a very broad term ranging as it does from 'having sex' – participating in sexual intercourse for reproduction – to the relational dimension which is an expression of love or pleasure or both.

So it follows that the range of issues associated with sexual ethics are equally broad. There are, however, two important considerations which this book will touch on in every chapter. First, is it possible to define human sexual identity? Second, what constraints, if any, should be placed on sexual behaviour?

1 Sexual identity

Is there such a thing as a 'typical man' or a 'typical woman'? Are there characteristics of men and of women which, regardless of time and place, remain *essentially* the same? To what extent would you agree with Daphne Hampson's description of men:

1 They appear, to women, so external. Men's talk is of cars, sport or computers ... Men seem to have no easy intercourse with others across boundaries, in the way that most women take for granted. The sole close relationship which most men have seems to be with their partner. Male
5 relationships tend to be competitive and concerned with honour. Men wish not to become entangled and not to let down the mask themselves. Male hierarchy gives the impression of being an attempt to keep others at bay; to control them so that they are not a threat and do not come too close.

D Hampson After Christianity (1996) p115

If human relationships are to be satisfying, happy and enduring there can be nothing more important than establishing just what it means to be human and how men and women should treat each other. It was not so long ago that it was permissible to buy and sell humans as slaves because in the mind of society they were not considered people but animals. The logic which was applied to the abolition of slavery has also to be applied to women and the birth of a movement which has transformed almost every aspect of Western society today: **feminism**.

In its narrow sense feminism is about women: women's rights and the perception and role of women in society. But any change in the way in which women see themselves and want to be seen by men cannot occur without a substantial shift in the way in which men understand themselves and their relationship with women. Feminism in its widest sense is characteristic of late 20th century Western culture's understanding of *all* human relationships. It affects every aspect of society from the ethics of reproduction and sexual intercourse to education, business, social structures, government, race and homosexuality.

The impact of feminism is often considered to be a **paradigm shift** – in other words, a major change in the way in which society forms its values and beliefs. Feminism has inspired new literary, dramatic forms and media as well as challenging some of the fundamental theological beliefs of the Christian church. Chapter 3 reviews the current debates, but other chapters on marriage (Chapter 5) and the family (Chapter 8) also consider the impact of feminism in these areas.

Feminism has created a climate of rapidly changing views about sexual identity. Another phenomenon in the new Western millennium is the increasing acceptability of **homosexuality**. The issue of homosexuality is much more than society allowing same-sex relationships but also entails a revolutionary new way of thinking about all sex and relationships. Symbolically, many reject the use of the term homosexuality and prefer instead to think in terms of being 'queer'. **Queer theory** suggests that there can be no hard and fast boundaries about what is or is not a legitimate sexual relationship and no institution has the right to impose its views on others; being queer is the freedom to define oneself according to one's nature, whatever that might be. Chapter 4 considers this issue in detail.

2 Liberty

So, if the issues raised above are to do with identity, where does morality fit in? By morality we mean rules and principles which restrain or permit forms of behaviour. In societies where there are many conflicting moral views this can be complex. Take the following example:

I The Bishop of Bristol has given his public support to the Revd Peter Stone, who is seeking a sex change (gender redesignation) through surgery. He will be known in the future as the Revd Carol Stone.

Doctors have diagnosed Mr Stone as having a gender dysmorphia, a
5 medical condition in which the sufferer feels trapped in a body of the wrong sex. 'I don't like the words "sex change" because it's not. It's just basically putting my heart and my head together with the rest of my body.'

The bishop acknowledged the steep learning curve he had been through
10 on the subject of trans-sexuality, but concluded, 'As far as I could see, there was no ecclesiastical law why he should not continue to be a priest

in the Church of England. I don't believe there's a moral issue here: this
is a medical condition and can be dealt with medically, now.'

Church Times 23 June 2000

What is interesting about the bishop's response here is that he does
not consider the issue to be one which involves any direct
considerations of morality. He is instructed by what scientists say is the
man's problem and he has then seen solution largely in terms of
medicine not Christian morality.

But for others this simply assumes that medicine is independent
from morality. For example, those who hold that ethics should be
based on some form of natural law, have particularly strong moral
views on different means of **reproduction**, the use of contraception
and human cloning (see Chapter 7). But even allowing the man to
have his sex change presumes a utilitarian morality which considers it
to be in his best interests to do so. In fact, it is really the contingencies
or side effects – his family, friends, life as a priest – which, in utilitarian
terms (the greatest happiness of the greatest number), appear to
determine what he should do.

For many in the West, however, the question whether he should or
should not have the operation is not one on which we should voice an
opinion because it is an entirely personal matter. For those who hold
that view, and it is one which democracies in the West have
increasingly adopted, the principle being referred to here is the one
of **liberty**.

The liberty principle can be expressed in many different ways, but
it is classically set out in J S Mill's influential essay *On Liberty* (1859).
Some of the key ideas of liberalism, which concern sexual ethics and
in particular the place of legislation are:

● That by allowing each person to adopt their own lifestyle they and
society 'flourish'.
● That a person should be considered to be ruler over their own body.
● That the state, society and others should not interfere in an adult
person's private relationships, even if this is harmful to themselves.
● That consenting adults may behave as they wish if and only if it causes
no harm to the wider community.

The significance of these notions should not be underestimated.
They may account, for instance, for why **cohabitation** is considered by
many to be an expression of personal freedom and lifestyle choice
and a valid replacement from the constraints of marriage (see
Chapter 6). Those who adopt the liberty principle as the basis for a
tolerant and civilised society may find that they have to give assent to
forms of relationships which personally they find unacceptable.
Increasingly for many there is no debate about homosexuality; it is
simply a lifestyle choice and the law should acknowledge it to be so.

Nevertheless, even a libertarian stance has to draw lines. If, for instance, there is empirical evidence (factual data) that homosexuality causes harm to society, offends the majority, or is a threat to children then, as Chapter 4 explores, there are good grounds for legislation to outlaw certain forms of sexual behaviour.

So in conclusion, the issues raised by sex and relationships question what it means to live fully as human beings and what we permit so that society may flourish.

2 Sex and gender

1 Nature-nurture

In 1792, **Mary Wollstonecraft (1759–1799)**, one of the founders of modern feminist thinking, wrote the following:

> 1 The prevailing opinion, that woman was created for man, may have its rise from Moses's poetical story; yet, as very few, it is presumed, who have bestowed any serious thought on the subject, ever supposed that Eve was, literally speaking, one of Adam's ribs, the deduction must be
> 5 allowed to fall to the ground; or, only be so far admitted as it proves that man, from the remotest antiquity, found it convenient to exert his strength to subjugate his companion, and have his invention to show that she ought to have her neck bent under the yoke, because the whole creation was only created for his convenience or pleasure.
>
> M Wollstonecraft *A Vindication of the Rights of Woman* (1792)

The surprisingly modern insight of Mary Wollstonecraft's reflection shows her understanding that the biblical writer's motives are the result of his cultural background. Sexual identity, as she makes clear, is to do with relationships, power and our perception of each other. Eve is what she is not because she has been created that way, but because she has been *nurtured* and shaped by Adam's expectations.

Since Wollstonecraft's time one of the major characteristics of Western society has been the attempt to understand more exactly the role of men and women. The process is complex. On the one hand, modern understanding of biology has effectively exploded many of the myths of the past as pre-scientific explanations to justify social custom. On the other hand, the results of anthropology, social history and psychology have suggested that 'sexuality' is a very broad term referring to the values, roles and attitudes which a society holds about men and women. The controversial philosopher **Michel Foucault (1926–1984)** even argued that the idea of 'sexuality' is a modern invention (see below, pages 14–17) designed to exercise political power over different members of society.

The argument has taken many twists and turns over the past 200 years, but in essence it is whether men and women are different because of fundamental biological differences (**nature**), or whether culture, economic forces and prevailing expectations have **nurtured** or **socialised** the roles into which males and females fall. The tension is therefore between **sex** – the biological or physical distinctions between **male** and **female**, and **gender** – the cultural classification between **masculine** and **feminine** characteristics.

2 Sex and gender

> **KEY ISSUE**
>
> ● Is it possible to define what constitutes 'normal' sexual behaviour?

The feminist writer Ann Oakley writes:

> Much of the confusion in the debate about sex roles comes from the fact that we tend to speak of 'sex differences' when we are really talking about differences of gender. Because of this the rationale of a society based on liberation from conventional gender roles is written off as an impossibility.
>
> A Oakley *Sex, Gender and Society* (1985) p189

It has become almost a commonplace among many that gender is therefore an entirely separate acquired characteristic from biological sex. Many quote Simone de Beauvoir's (1908–1986) well-known statement:

> One is not born, but rather becomes, a woman.
>
> S de Beauvoir *The Second Sex* (1949) p 249

But the matter is not easily resolved. Customs associated with gender may well be cultural, such as clothes, hairstyle and social roles, but writers, both ancient and modern, have long suggested that the way in which societies are constructed in terms of morality, law and religion is based on an *objective* understanding of the individual sexual body.

Set out below are three very different viewpoints each concerned with the **aetiology** or the origins of human sexuality. Each of the representative examples within these categories is controversial but influential.

● The biological viewpoint thinks in terms of genes and hormones
● The psychological viewpoint thinks in terms of mental development
● The theological viewpoint thinks in terms of human spirituality.

a) Biology of sex

We shall begin with an account of the biological sexual development of the human foetus. The first important observation is that it is only after a period of foetal development in the womb that it is possible to say whether the emergent baby will be male or female. In some cases, where the process is confused or distorted, the baby may only be considered *more* male or *less* female without satisfying either category completely. Knowledge of this kind has helped society to understand that for some people their sexual identity may not fall easily into the biological norms.

i Male/female foetal development

Ann Oakley summarises the following process of foetal sexual development (*Sex, Gender and Society* Chapter 1):

● At conception the genetic material from the male's sperm decides the sex of the child. The mother's egg contains only X. If the sperm contains an X chromosome then the embryo will be female (XX), if it contains a Y chromosome the result will a male embryo (XY).
● Up to seven weeks after fertilisation, the sex organs of both sexes are based on identical physical development. An external opening leads to the bladder and to internal genitalia and 'genital tubercle' – at this stage a rudimentary penis or clitoris.
● After seven weeks the tubercle enlarges for the male to form a penis and for the female it ceases to develop and becomes the clitoris. The skin round the urogenital opening which for the male had passed through the penis, develops in the female to become the labia.
● At this stage sexual development is determined by the hormones released by the gonads or testes in the foetus containing the Y chromosome (the male). The female combination of XX genes releases the appropriate hormone at a much later stage. Without the release of

the hormone even a foetus with XY chromosomes will develop as a female. An intersexual child and then later as an adult, might therefore have the gonads (testes or ovaries) of a male but secondary genitalia of a female (i.e. a vagina and not a penis).

● At birth male and female babies may vary in size and weight – in the west baby boys tend to be heavier and longer. Somatotype or external physical looks between men and women often depend on ethnic background. Amongst the Manus of the Admiralty Islands, for instance, there is no major somatotype differences between children, and men and women are both muscular and broad shouldered.

● The differentiation between X and Y chromosomes also determine future physical defects. The Y chromosome accounts for 62 disorders (from haemophilia to colour blindness) because these disorders are contained in a defective X chromosome. For females their other X chromosome can cancel out any abnormalities, but the male Y chromosome is unable to do this.

ii Difference

But we must be careful not to assume that this is an entirely objective account. Oakley has her own agenda. From her description of the biological *differences* she deduces that it is men who have developed their characteristics from women. Rather than being the 'weaker sex' research has indicated that women are more likely to live longer than men:

1   How can these differences be explained? A breakdown of the mortality figures shows that men are more susceptible than women to some hazards. Where death is due to non-infectious diseases, some of the excess in male deaths is due to the preponderance in male diseases
5   and defects transmitted by the sex-linked mutant genes, However, epilepsy, for example, has roughly the same incidence in both sexes, but the death rate from it is about 30% higher in males. Recent research suggests that one of the female sex hormones, progesterone, may be an anti-convulsive and sedative agent, so some of the female's superior
10   survival capacity may come from her hormones.

A Oakley *Sex, Gender and Society* (1985) p34

It also appears from research that females live longer and are less likely to die from accidents in the home, but even though Oakley concludes that 'no satisfactory explanation of this sex difference in vulnerability has yet been given' we can see that she is keen to assert that women are biologically 'superior' in some ways to men and that men are prone to certain 'defects'.

iii Criticisms

Despite Oakley's own claim that sex and gender are entirely different categories she herself moves from objective biological observation to value-judgements. The problem with scientific observation of this kind is that it often appears to have the weight of objective neutrality. But, as Thomas Kuhn, the philosopher of science, noted about scientific 'facts', they are all 'value laden' for there is a great deal more at stake than mere fact. Inevitably the interpretation of data will depend on the culture, other beliefs and existing scientific ideas.

b) Psychology of sex

Sigmund Freud (1856–1939) was one of the founders of psychoanalysis. His significance for the question of the relationship between sex and gender lies at the very heart of much of his analysis and claim that a great many of our psychological problems can be explained because of sexual traumas through conflict caused between the natural sex drive (the **libido**) and external social events (such as an extremely repressive sexual upbringing, for example).

i 'Anatomy is destiny'
Freud was one of the first to equate the biological features of sex with the psychological description of a person's gender. Freud argued that the psychological development of a child will *inevitably* determine a boy or girl's gender characteristics; or as Freud famously described this process, 'anatomy is destiny'.

ii Ego development
The crucial stages for a child's character development take place between the ages of 0 and 5. During this time the 'ego', or conscious self, evolves in direct correlation to biological growth. So at the 'oral' stage a child depends physically on its mother for milk, but *psychologically* the ego develops dependency, or at the next stage (the 'anal') the psychological state is to be tidy, associated with the physical acts of excretion and so on. 'Normal' boys and girls pass through these stages and by the end of the period at the start of 'latency' each has acquired their set gender types. Any factor that upsets this process will also confuse the resultant gender.

iii Oedipus and castration complex
At the first two stages (oral and anal) boys and girls *both* enjoy the same sexual experiences which are entirely focused on the mother. Suddenly, however the boy becomes aware of his mother as a sexual being and wishes to sleep with her. He is jealous of his father's relationship with his mother and wishes to kill him. But he also realises through observation that his father has a penis and his mother has not. He concludes, therefore, that as his mother has no penis his father has castrated her and could do the same to him. Out of fear he learns to respect his father and repress his sexual feelings for his mother. When he reaches sexual adulthood he will learn to direct them to his wife.

iv Penis envy

Girls do not pass through the Oedipus moment in the same way, although the experience of castration is encountered but with modified results. Girls, like boys, become aware of their sexual relationships with their mothers and fathers. The realisation that they have no penis whereas their brothers or male friends do have one brings an important, though painful, break in their dependency on their mother and transference of sexual affinity to the father. Girls often have tense relationships with their mothers whom they hold to be responsible for their castration. Their penis envy is resolved when they have children: the baby is sexually the penis replacement.

v Super-ego and gender

Freud did not support the androgyny view that men and women are essentially the same. The trauma of the Oedipus moment forces the ego to adopt its own moral perspective which it does by replacing the agency of mother and father, this he called the **super-ego**. The super-ego or conscience is the extension of the ego which dictates the gender role of men and women. The masculine traits are according to Freud: competitive, hierarchical, respect for authority, conformists, sense of justice. The feminine traits are: maternal, submissive, sacrificial, co-operative.

vi Criticisms of Freud

Criticism of Freud might include the following:

- His gender types conform to typical Victorian expectations of the time.
- He has too deterministic a view of sex and gender. Gender is more open-ended.
- He has little evidence for the Oedipus moment (on which his theory depends).
- He fails to allow for cultural expectations and influences on the super-ego via parental agency
- He puts too much emphasis on the penis as a symbol of power.
- He falsely makes men morally superior to women.

c) Theology of sex

Up until the 20th century, Western Christian tradition has been dominated by a view of human sexuality developed in extraordinary detail by the North African bishop and scholar, **St Augustine of Hippo (354–430 CE)**. Augustine's own life and conversion to Christianity (late August 386 CE) played a vital role in his understanding of sex and its central place in human experience and salvation. Before his conversion he had, like many young men of his class and background, kept a concubine (or mistress) and fathered a child. Unlike some of his Christian teachers he was not ignorant of sex nor did he find it unpleasurable. On the contrary, it was because the libido was so real and independent from his own rational will that he came, in time, to equate it with the darker side of human nature, namely sin.

i Sex and the fall

Augustine took a fairly literal view of Genesis and in particular the story of the Fall (Genesis 3) where Adam led on by Eve and tempted by the snake caused both to discover their nakedness. This Augustine understood to mean that whereas Adam and Eve had until that point enjoyed a sexual relationship as friends, a relationship which would include the production of children (God had, after all, commanded them to be 'fruitful and occupy the earth' Genesis 1:28), their disobedience was at once forever linked with their own realisation of their sexual bodies.

By the time Augustine wrote his greatest work, *The City of God* (413–426 CE), his argument with the Pelagians (who rejected the idea of original sin) confirmed his belief that the sex drive and death were to be considered the punishment for human rebellion; both perpetually reminded men and women of their distorted, sinful will and loss of harmony between body and soul.

ii Concupiscence

But Augustine did not despise sex and marriage. At a time when virginity was often considered to be the only truly Christian way of life, Augustine regarded marriage as a reflection of the original and natural state of Adam and Eve in the Garden of Eden (see Chapter 5, page 78). His view varied considerably from his contemporaries such as Gregory of Nyssa, Ambrose and Jerome – for whom marriage and sex were incompatible with the perfect state of Paradise.

Augustine's theology, therefore, in his remarkable, frank book *Confessions* (398 CE) develops very much what St Paul had described in his letter to the Romans, almost four hundred years before:

> 1 I do not understand my own actions. For I do not do what I want, but I do the very thing I hate. Now if I do what I do not want, I agree that the law is good. So then it is no longer I that do it, but sin which dwells within me...For I do not do the good I want, but the evil I do not want
> 5 is what I do. Now if I do what I do not want, it is no longer I that do it, but sin which dwells within me. ...but I see in my members another law at war with the law of my mind and making me captive to the law of sin which dwells in my members. Wretched man that I am! Who will deliver me from this body of death?
>
> Romans 7:15-24

Although Augustine held a Platonic dualistic view that the body and soul are separate, he rejected the Manichean (an extreme Christian 3rd-century heretical sect) argument that the body is in itself sinful. It is not the body which is sinful, but the rebellious *will*. The will constantly craves power, food, money and above all sexual intercourse. This is **concupiscence**. Ideally, Augustine imagined, sex would only take place when a man and woman considered the time was right to have a child. Then, by exerting his will over his body the man could summon an erection but without lust in order to have sex. In reality what actually happens is that spontaneous erections, wet dreams and loss of control during sexual orgasm all reveal the presence of concupiscence and the lack of control that the soul has over sin (see *City of God* 14:16–25). Even impotence or lack of libido is a sign that the body is able to mock the will.

iii Male and female difference

Augustine also resisted other contemporaries in their explanation of the woman's subordinate relationship with man. He rejected the interpretation of Genesis by the Jewish philosopher Philo of Alexandria (*c*20 BCE – *c*50 CE), who blamed Adam's sin on Eve's evil nature, and instead argued that men and women were created equal, though different:

> So God created man in his own image, in the image of God he created him; male and female he created them.
>
> Genesis 1:27

As both male and female are created in the image of God, both share in God's *rational* nature. To that extent men and women are equal. But despite this, a woman's body is *symbolically* different from a man's. For just as human reason is designed both to obey God and to rule over the animal world, so a woman's body suggests that she is to be ruled over by the man to be his 'help mate'. Thus the taking of the rib from Adam (Genesis 2:22–24) illustrates that although both share the same spiritual nature, Eve is subordinate to man in *practical* reason and in everyday practical affairs. Her role as helpmate is as a wife and a mother.

> 1 And just as in man's soul there are two forces, one which is dominant because it deliberates and one which obeys because it is subject to such guidance, in the same way, in the physical sense, woman has been made for man. In her mind and her rational intelligence she has a nature the
> 5 equal of man's, but in sex she is physically subject to him in the same way as our natural impulses need to be subjected to the reasoning power of the mind, in order that the actions to which they lead may be inspired by the principles of good conduct.
>
> Augustine *Confessions* 13:32

So, although a woman is subservient to the man Augustine had tried hard to avoid the traditional depiction of her as the temptress and agent of the devil. Nevertheless, in so far as a woman is defined by her physical body, she is inferior to the man. Augustine refers to St Paul's letter to the Corinthians, where Paul writes:

> For a man ought not to cover his head, since he is the image and glory of God; but woman is the glory of man...That is why a woman ought to have a veil on her head, because of the angels.
>
> *I Corinthians I I:7, I0*

Paul draws an analogy between Moses' experience of God on Mount Sinai (Exodus 34:33–35), after which he had to cover his face because his nature had been completed by his encounter. In the same way, the reason why a woman must wear a veil is a sign that she has been completed through her relationship with her husband, who is the uncorrupted image of God.

iv Thomas Aquinas

Augustine's model of male–female spiritual equivalence but rational subordination is developed in a slightly different way by the medieval philosopher and theologian **Thomas Aquinas (c1225–1274)**. Whereas Augustine's ideas were based on the mind–body dualism of Plato, Aquinas developed the function of the female body by developing the ideas of **Aristotle (384–322 BCE)**. The effect of Aquinas' adaptation of Augustine is particularly important for the view that a women must be, by nature, the passive helpmate to her husband. There are two important alterations to Augustine's model.

Firstly, Aquinas, far more than Augustine, saw in man the active role of the one who, because he was created before woman, took on God's creative role in the world to subdue it and multiply. Just as God is the first vital principle of the universe, man (in the image of God) is the first principle of the earth.

> For man is the beginning and end of woman; as God is the beginning and end of every creature.
>
> Aquinas *Summa Theologica* I, 93.4
>
> quoted by G Lloyd in *Feminist Theology: A Reader* by A Loades (1991), p 95

Secondly, it was believed that in man's sperm or 'seed' were all the ingredients for new human life; the woman provided the right environment for germination and growth to take place. In Aristotelian terms, therefore, a woman's natural and primary *telos* or purpose is in **generation**, as a child bearer and mother. Aquinas also adopted Aristotle's notion that a woman's inferiority is confirmed by the fact that a female foetus receives her soul after 90 days, whereas the male is given his after 40 days.

Aquinas' biological account of gender differences suggested that woman is by her dependency on man (as suggested by the taking of the rib from Adam in Genesis 2:21–22) less rational at the level of practical earthly reason. Only through marriage is a woman able to gain this aspect of her which she is lacking, just as humans through worship receive God's grace.

> Good order would have been wanting in the human family if some were not governed by others wiser than themselves. So by such a kind of subjection woman is naturally subject to man, because in man, the discretion of reason predominates.
>
> Aquinas *Summa Theologica* I, 92.1
> quoted by G Lloyd in *Feminist Theology: A Reader* by A Loades (1991), p 95

v Criticisms of Augustine and Aquinas

Despite the efforts of Augustine and Aquinas to place men and women at the same spiritual level while still accounting for their differences, criticisms of their views today include:

- An overemphasis on the relationship between sin and sex.
- Spiritual equality between men and women is not enough. Modern Christianity takes account of feminist experience where women are considered to be equal with men.
- Too much concern is placed on reason as that which defines humans.
- Rationality is defined only in male hierarchical terms. Feminists today offer different interpretations of rationality which are based on relationship not power.
- Modern Christians use different biological and psychological starting points rather than Aristotle and Plato.
- Modern Biblical criticism suggests that the Genesis stories should not be treated as historical events, but rather as metaphorical stories.

d) Narrative of sexuality

All the views outlined above seek to explain human sexuality in terms of historical, psychological, biological origins or aetiology. But do they actually do that? Looking at them again we see that each was really a narrative or story to justify a particular view. For instance, if we think of ourselves, our school or our nation we understand its identity is created not at a founding moment, but through its history and development. Its identity at any particular moment will depend on a range of political, social and scientific influences. This way of thinking rejects the idea that there can be any fixed or *objective* sexual nature, no right or wrong sexuality.

i The birth of sexuality

This way of thinking has been developed by the writings of the controversial but influential French philosopher **Michel Foucault** (1926–1984), whose notion of *sexuality* we have looked at briefly above. Foucault's startling conclusion is that sexuality is a modern invention. By this he doesn't mean that humans have not thought and discussed sex, but that thinking in terms of having a distinct, objective sexual identity is a Western phenomenon which has evolved over the past two hundred years.

Foucault's ideas are developed in his three-volume *The History of Sexuality* (1976–1984). However, he does not look at history in a conventional way as he is not interested so much in the causes of sex as the way in which the ideas and practices have emerged in society.

> Sexuality must not be thought of as a kind of natural given ... It is the name that can be given to a historical construct: not a furtive reality that is difficult to grasp, but a great surface network.

> M Foucault *The History of Sexuality: The Will to Knowledge* (1979) p105

Foucault has his own agenda: what he wants to illustrate is that the modern period, since the late 18th century, has been a distortion of earlier human sexual experience. This distortion has arisen due firstly to an obsession with wanting to classify everything into categories or 'species' (as he calls them) and secondly, the desire to get people to conform to these categories. By inventing a category called 'human sexuality' society has developed an enormously powerful and repressive tool to order people into conformity.

ii Genealogy and discourse
Foucault therefore rejected any claim that there could be an aetiology of sex; instead he suggests that we should think instead of a **genealogy** of sex. Genealogy is looking at the way societies have developed their own identities through what Foucault calls their **discourses**. A discourse is a combination of two elements. Firstly, the way a group of people think and talk about themselves (their narrative), and secondly the practices which follow from these ideas.

Sexual discourses cannot be static or fixed. Humans are forever defining and redefining their relationships with each other. What we see in history is that although some discourses come to dominate more than others, sexual discourses were always part of a range of other elements such as health, politics, religion and philosophy.

iii Power and knowledge
Foucault's analysis of recent history is that sexual identity has fallen into the hands of the so-called 'expert'. Here Foucault makes an important distinction between what he calls the *ars erotica* of the ancient and eastern worlds and the repressive *scientia sexualis* (sexual sciences) of the west. The *ars erotica* are the practices of human sexuality as pleasure which do not lead to the repressive control of external institutions or ideologies. But the modern *scientia sexualis* by contrast insists that pleasure is a form of knowledge which can be defined objectively, regulated and imposed universally.

How has this come about? The first major development has been the Christian churches' view that the fallen and sinful human state is universal. As we have seen (page 11) both Augustine and Aquinas equated human sexuality with the practice of sin. Here are the beginnings of the *scientia sexualis*. But Christianity adds a second vital element, the need to confess one's sin in order to become normal or good. Pleasure is now to be experienced through the practice of confession not sex itself.

But as the Christian religious discourse diminished from the 18th century it was replaced by a number of competing non-religious, rational and scientific discourses which, in the process of categorising all forms of knowledge, also found themselves defining sex.

The new discourses of the biologist, psychologist, lawyer and educationalist have each imposed its view of what 'normal' human sexuality is. Freud is a very good example, as we have seen, of one person who attempted to give a coherent account of human development in biological and psychological terms almost entirely in terms of sexuality (see page 9). But the Freudian discourse was not entirely motivated by the desire for objective knowledge but by the power to bring the patient back into socially accepted norms. So, although Freud sought to liberate individuals from their fears and anxieties, paradoxically he was at the same time also reinforcing repressive sexual practices.

At the heart of all the discourses of the *scientia sexualis*, Foucault argues, is still the desire to use the confession to control and have power over the individual. Sadly, rather than releasing the individual and empowering him or her to express their own pleasures, the *scientia sexualis* have created a deeply repressed and sexually confused culture.

iv Narrative freedom

What does Foucault hope to achieve by his genealogical approach to sexuality? We have seen that Foucault is impressed by the *ars erotica* of other cultures and the ancient world. But he is also indebted to the visionary and highly original philosophy of Friederich Nietzsche (1844–1900) whose understanding of the human condition was based not on submission to a god, or ideology or natural law but the belief that humans are the source of their own creative power. Nietzsche's notion of the **will to power** is employed by Foucault to mean that to be truly human one can and must act creatively and without repressive constraint of any one dominant discourse.

Foucault's ideas have been developed by his followers into what is sometimes called **queer theory**, where the term 'queer' is intentionally used to challenge existing fixed views of sexuality. Queer theory has been particularly significant in the emergence of homosexuality and a consciously different discourse of human sexuality (see page 46 below).

v Criticisms of Foucault

● Although Foucault's argument appears to give considerable freedom to feminist and gay movements his ideas also suggest that they may be no more than a passing phase in our larger social narrative. There is no such thing, for instance, as gay or lesbian identity.

● Foucault's view of human behaviour has few safeguards. If there are no ethical or social absolutes how do we protect against exploitation? An ethic based on power appears to lack many human virtues such as love and compassion.

● Foucault's survey of ancient Roman and Greek cultures did not reveal societies where any form of sexual behaviour was acceptable. Social and ideological constraints set clear guidelines.

● Foucault's analysis may be said merely to reflect a Western cultural phase, a temporary loss of confidence in traditional institutions. He does not represent what a great deal of the world thinks about sexual matters.

Answering structured and essay questions

Essay skills

You must be careful not to make sweeping and generalised statements. Oakley, Augustine/Aquinas and Foucault all represent distinct ways of understanding human sexuality from particular viewpoints. You should therefore be clear that there are many other feminist views, Christian views and post-modern views. Essays on Augustine and Aquinas should recognise that neither writers had the same kind of biological knowledge we have today. As both men rely on non-Christian philosophers for authority think how their ideas might be adapted in the light of recent biological and psychological thinking. You will need also to define your terms: sex, sexuality, gender can be used in different and overlapping ways. Don't forget you are testing these ideas and that the rightness or wrongness of your answer really depends on how well you present your argument. There are no set answers.

You may wish to use the following diagram for the basis for your notes. Try and indicate how one area of investigation has affected the other. Add criticisms. As you read other chapters in this book you may wish to add other examples into each category.

Summary diagram

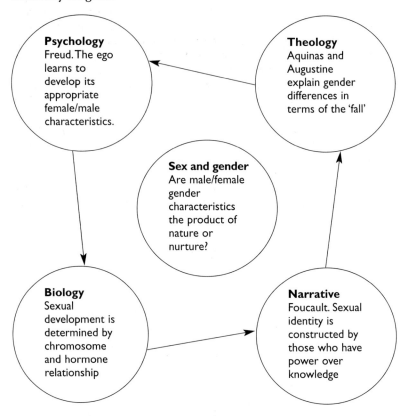

Questions

1. **a)** Explain why Augustine thought men and women were different.
    b) 'Augustine's view of male and female nature is deeply flawed'. Discuss.
2. **a)** What did Freud mean by the phrase 'anatomy is destiny'?
    b) To what extent can we say that gender is entirely due to nurture not to nature?
3. 'If queer theory is right then the idea of gender is meaningless'. Discuss.
4. 'Augustine offers a much more satisfactory view of human sexuality than Freud.' Discuss.
5. 'Other than some obvious biological differences, men and women are essentially the same.' Discuss.

3 Feminisms

1 Seeing the world in gendered terms

1   Feminist discourse has given us a stance from which to 'read' the past. What appeared unremarkable is now seen as culturally specific: the product of a system called patriarchy. The world is shown to be gendered. There is a construction of masculinity and equally of
5   femininity.

D Hampson After Christianity (1996) p87

Feminism has changed the way we see the present, but it has also made us rethink and review how men and women existed in the past. However, although we tend to talk of feminism as if it were a coherent and single movement, feminism covers a range of different ideas and developments often quite different from each other. For instance, women who have fought for equal rights may not regard themselves as feminists and indeed are not considered to be feminists by others because they have no distinctive view of women.

i Philosophical inspiration

An aim of feminism is to ensure that the voice of women is heard and incorporated into philosophical, moral and political debate. Inevitably therefore each stage of feminism has absorbed and used contemporary ideas. The earliest feminists were inspired by the social upheavals of the French Revolution (1789) and **enlightenment** philosophers such as **Immanuel Kant (1724–1804)** and then **John Stuart Mill (1806–1873)**. More radical movements in the latter part of the 20th century have found inspiration in the philosophical writings of Karl Marx's collaborator **Frederich Engels (1820–1895)**, the visionary **Friederich Nietzsche (1844–1900)** and existentialist **Jean-Paul Sartre (1905–1980)**. With the accumulation of women's writing and philosophical reflections the most recent phase of feminism has developed its own particular terms of reference independent from the male philosophers who inspired it in the past.

ii Sexism
Many institutions, the workplace, and the media are consciously or unconsciously sexist in spite of the impact that feminism has had on Western culture. Women are discriminated against in all kinds of ways. Take the following example by Juliet Mitchell (*The Longest Revolution* 1984):

1 The daughter of the Queen of England married a commoner. Her father, who himself was not the king, gave her away to her husband, to whose place of residence she then removed. Princess Anne, as she herself said, is an 'old-fashioned' girl and she embellished the proceedings by
5 promising to honour and obey her husband.

What sexist attitudes does this illustrate?

● A religion which reinforces the notion that women are subservient to men.
● A view of marriage which sees women to be the object of exchange from man to man.
● A view of society which is patriarchal and hierarchical symbolised by a monarchy.
● A view which illustrates how women themselves are often unaware that they are responsible for reinforcing sexist attitudes.

iii Feminisms
There is no single coherent system called 'feminism'. The many different experiences of women have inevitably led to a wide range of different perceptions of what it means to be a woman. Even so, all feminisms share in common the desire to liberate and value women from sexism.

2 Liberal feminisms

KEY ISSUE

● Is equality with men all that women want in their relationships and in the workplace?

The earliest phase of feminism was influenced by the enlightenment philosophers who argued that morality is not derived from God or built into nature but in human reason alone. Kant in particular made the simple but highly significant proposal that if humans are all characterised by their rationality then it follows that whatever differences there may be between us, we are bound by a common universal human rational will. In what he termed the **categorical imperative** he stated that what I would wish for myself is only morally acceptable if I can will it for all others. A second version of the categorical imperative, sometimes called the **practical imperative**, states that we should never treat people as a means to an end but an end in themselves. These two notions form the basis of liberal feminism.

a) Reason and rights

In the rapidly changing societies of the era of the French Revolution, women writers of the period, notably **Mary Wollstonecraft** in Britain and **Olympe de Gouges** (*Declaration of the Rights of Women Citizens* 1791) in France, argued logically that if civil rights were being extended to all men (regardless of class or belief) then they should include rights for women. Anything less would be to treat women as means and not as ends in themselves (i.e. as a form of slavery) and fail to apply moral duties to *all* people (men *and* women).

The liberal feminism of Wollstonecraft does not argue that the roles of men and women should be the same, but that women should have the same opportunities (to work, to vote, to be educated) and the same rights as men. After two hundred years most of these aims have been fulfilled and the number of jobs that are barred to women – even in the armed forces – are shrinking all the time.

b) Liberation and freedom of choice

Another characteristic of the enlightenment philosophers was that reason offered the opportunity to reject anything which could not adequately be explained in rational terms. Tradition, superstition and religion cannot in themselves be sufficient reason to justify legislation. Perhaps the most influential statement of what we might call the liberal principle is enshrined by John Stuart Mill in *On Liberty* (1859) and in the utilitarian principle of the greatest happiness of the greatest number (men and women). The principle is essentially non-judgemental and states that whatever people believe on a personal and private basis is no concern of the state. The function of the state is to maximise personal freedom and only to limit certain behaviour when it interferes with the freedom of others and reduces the overall happiness of society.

The classical liberal position is expressed jointly by John Stuart Mill in his *The Subjection of Women* (1869) and also by his partner (and later wife) **Harriet Taylor (1805–1858)** in her *Enfranchisement of Women* (1851). Their essays are significant for their disagreement about the nature of women's liberation. Mill held that even though women are less capable than men they should be given the freedom to exercise their talents to the best of their ability. Mill rejected the naturalistic claim that the woman, as wife, has a duty to minister to the needs of the family. For the utilitarian principle to work all members of society should work for the greatest good. Giving women the ability to vote is symbolic of the role of women in a liberal society.

Taylor went further. She stated that the inequalities between men and women derive from tradition and custom: once women are given equal education, placed in the workforce and share in the running of the state, then it will be apparent that women are equal to men in all these aspects. Taylor's argument hints at one of the essential weaknesses of the liberal model: freedom of choice is not sufficient in itself in order for women to discover their own distinctive identity. For Taylor this meant that if women are to be true partners with men they must have the opportunity to earn their own income independently from their husbands.

c) Liberation and welfare

Since the 1960s feminists have had to resolve the tension between the woman as mother and career woman. At first, the new liberated woman was encouraged to be both – as Taylor had suggested a century before. But the 'superwoman' model of the 1960–1970s proved an impossible aspiration. Despite countless magazine articles claiming that women could do both for many it was simply another form of slavery. The most recent phase of the liberal feminist movement calls for a return to the liberal principle of social reform and to ensure that the state provides for women adequate child-care, flexible working hours, maternity leave, etc. Classical liberal feminism has given way to a welfare liberal model. This phase of liberal feminism recognises that giving men and women the equality of opportunity is not enough. The classical utilitarian model must also give way to a form of preference utilitarianism which accounts for the different preferences of men and women.

For example, Betty Frieden in her important book *The Second Stage* (1981), argues that preference liberal feminism is only a stage in the historical development of women in society. Will the next stage be an androgynous one of 'true' equality between men and women where gender differences will simply have melted away?

d) Criticisms of liberal feminisms

Even though liberal feminism has a number of forms, its aims are sufficiently similar for the following criticisms to apply generally:

i Androcentric

The earlier phase of liberal feminism looked for equality for women and men in a man's world. Wollstonecraft wanted girls to be educated in the same way as boys. In other words the desire to give women rights and opportunities are male-centred or 'androcentric' and expressed in terms of male values and virtues. True liberation has to acknowledge that in some important areas men and women are different as defined by women not men.

ii Reason and rights are masculine

The enlightenment emphasis on the universal place of reason has been developed entirely in masculine terms. The contention here is that women's logic is more intuitive and co-operative whereas the kind of rationality which liberalism has accepted to be self-evident is male gender-specific: legalistic and hierarchical. In other words liberal feminism does not have a coherent idea of women's identity and adopts the male tendency to promote mental activity above emotion to be superior.

iii False duty

Many have argued that many women simply do not want to be 'like men'. They do not want to work and feel that their roles as wife and mother have been undermined by the implicit criticism (see Taylor above page 22) that if they do not work they have devalued themselves. Women do not have to be members of the public world to be good citizens.

iv Superficial

Many argue that liberalism only scratches the surface. True feminism needs to be far more revolutionary if real social justice is to be achieved. Feminism requires a complete reconstruction of society's consciousness. It is true that liberalism may have changed many important laws, but its founding principle has prohibited it from intruding into the private thoughts and values of individuals. Whilst liberalism continues in this form society will continue to be at heart sexist and prejudiced against women.

3 Social reconstruction feminisms

KEY ISSUE

● What kind of changes in society will be needed to abolish sexism?

The second form of feminism states that liberal feminism will ultimately fail in its aim to liberate women because society is, deep down, male and **patriarchal** (its values and structures are derived from the male point of view) and designed to fulfil the needs of men not women. There are two important philosophical influences here – Marxism and existentialism – both of which offer a radical reconstruction of society and its awareness of women.

a) Marxist feminism

Karl Marx (1818–1883) considered that history was divided between those who owned the means of production (the bourgeoisie) and those who were dependent on them (the proletariat). Without the ability to determine their own lives (especially as the result of industrialisation) the proletariat became slaves, exploited economically and spiritually. A central Marxist notion is that key moments in history are often determined by a few but quickly become in the minds of the many a fixed objective reality. This is **false consciousness**. False consciousness in feminist terms is the idea that women need to be dependent on men. The only means of destroying the false dualism between oppressed and oppressor is by a radical reconstruction of every aspect of social life. Feminism which has emerged from this way of thinking has had a powerful effect on modern Western society.

The work which continues to provide inspiration for radical feminists is by **Friedrich Engels (1820–1895)**, Marx's friend and supporter, in his *The Origin of the Family, Private Property, and the State* (1884). Engels argues that whereas in the past men and women enjoyed some degree of partnership, women in industrial society have become increasingly the object of men's power in the means of production (not just in child rearing but in all tasks associated with creating the family). Just as the bourgeoisie exploits the proletariat so men consider themselves as the owners of women – and this is true in every social class. Marxist feminists frequently describe the woman's role in terms of prostitution because she is sexually and economically exploited by men.

If Marxism advocates a revolutionary means to achieve justice and a society where all citizens are free from exploitation then the Marxist feminist also realises that true liberation for women comes when all existing economic social structures are deconstructed. The reconstructed society will be free from patriarchy, competition and capitalism. Only then can women (and men) enjoy full and satisfying relationships.

i Production

A major contribution of Marxist feminism has been to elevate the role of the woman in rearing and sustaining the family. Capitalism has tended to belittle the 'work' of the woman to be less valuable than the real work of men (or even women) for wages outside the home. In the past, in pre-industrial Europe, women and men worked with the common aim of sustaining the family. With industrialisation, the means of production moved outside the family into factories; whereas men were able, unencumbered with children, to work outside the home, women were left with the primary job of child rearing. The effect has been to devalue the woman's role, because she is not a wage earner and does not contribute publicly to society. But as Engels argues here, this is a very limited view of what production means:

1   According to the materialistic conception, the determining factor in
    history is, in the final instance, the production and reproduction of
    immediate life. This, again, is of two fold character: on the one side, the
    production of the means of existence, of food, clothing and shelter and
5   the tools necessary for that production; on the other side, the
    production of human beings themselves, the propagation of the species.
    The social organisation under which the people of a particular
    historical epoch live is determined by both kinds of production.

F Engels *The Origin of the Family, Private Property, and the State* (1884)
Preface

Modern feminist Marxists have argued that liberation for women should not confine a woman to a particular role – wage earner and child rearing are equally important and significant. The problem is caused by the capitalist environment which has set ideas about what constitutes useful work and liberal reforms which, though designed to protect women and children from exploitation, have in fact, made it harder for women to work as co-equals with men. When women have worked publicly their work has often been regarded as an extension of their family role as teachers, nurses, cleaners or secretaries and paid proportionally.

ii Socialisation of domestic work
One solution is for society to recognise the essential role a woman plays in the home and in the rearing of the family in society. In other words, work of this kind is not a private activity but should be recognised as an essential public contribution along with any other paid employment. The socialisation of the woman's role enables her to be placed as an equal with all other workers and gain the respect she deserves. Advocates urged the state to provide an allowance or welfare payment in recognition of the woman's role. Although this view is controversial amongst Marxist feminists nevertheless it inspired the 'wages for housework' campaign in the USA in the late 1960s.

iii Sexuality and pornography
The Marxist feminist does not have a particular view of what a woman ought to be like or whether she has a distinctive sexuality.

Relationships are considered almost entirely in terms of whether the economic conditions have exploited or enslaved. Marxist feminists today have concentrated on making radical inroads into the work place and for equal treatment such as pay and conditions. Engel's views on marriage and sexuality (see Chapter 5 pages 93–95) consider that all relationships under capitalism are bound to be unhappy and exploitative. We can see this in the way in which many aspects of media portray women as commodities to be acquired, adorned and used as sexual objects by men. Pornography is viewed as one of the worst aspects of a patriarchal and sexist society. Marxist feminists regard all these social aspects as forms of slavery and typical of capitalist societies where relationships have been reduced to buying and selling. However, Engel's view illustrates the hope that once economic freedom has been achieved then there will be equal respect between men and women; marriage will not be a form of institutionalised prostitution (i.e. slavery) but love between equals.

b) Existential feminism

Existentialism shares with Marxism the idea that humans can only really be fulfilled and happy when they act freely and in accordance with their true nature. But where it differs from the Marxist view is in its belief that humans are by nature productive beings – this limits both women and men. Existentialism is far more radical and argues that there is no intrinsic human nature. **Jean-Paul Sartre (1905–1980)** argued that humans are born with no predetermined nature – their physical existence (*en soi*) precedes their essence (*pour soi*). Essence or nature is developed by conscious free action. In Sartre's terms, an inauthentic life is where a person is unable to act freely or where they let themselves slip into a stereotypical role. This he calls bad faith (*mauvaise fois*). The implications for feminism at first seem to be clear:

● there is no predetermined female nature
● women are responsible for their actions just as much as men
● all social structures which inhibit women to exist authentic lives must be removed
● solidarity with others is achieved in the common authentic existence.

However, it is Sartre's life-long partner **Simone de Beauvoir (1908–1986)** who whilst sharing many of Sartre's philosophical ideals, reveals a major flaw in his way of thinking. Her hugely influential book *The Second Sex* (1949) acknowledges that women have allowed themselves for centuries to become the second sex and to act the role of the wife, the lover and the sex object according to the needs of men. Whilst they continue this form of bad faith they cannot live fully authentic and fulfilled lives. Woman's essence is defined by men for men and so they have falsely allowed their bodies to dictate their roles:

> The body is not enough to define her as a woman; there is no true living reality, except as manifested by the conscious individual through activities and in the bosom of a society.
>
> S de Beauvoir *The Second Sex* (1949) p685

But whilst this is true de Beauvoir also senses that women have become trapped by the deeper structures of society to become objects (like the rest of nature). Far from being equal with men in the existential quest, women are in an impossible position. They are not subjects, as men are, able to exercise freedom, but objects fixed by the weight of tradition. Change can only come from a collaborative effort of both men and women, not by transcending society, but by entering into it and working away until the structures of society make it possible for women to live their own authentic lives. One important aspect of de Beauvoir's utopian view is that she shows how even Sartre's existentialism unwittingly reveals a very male world view; of the egotistical, competitive individual challenging and attacking all that he sees. De Beauvoir's critique of Sartre reveals how deeply ingrained the male view of the world has become.

c) Criticisms of social reconstruction feminisms

Criticisms of Marxist and existentialist feminism include the following:

- Work as freedom: Many have suggested that giving women economic freedom and valuing their work in the family only tackles one aspect of the feminist agenda – it does not go far enough in considering the particular sexual needs and interests of women independent of their economic status.
- Private diversity: Some have argued that the Marxist feminist emphasis on the social and public value of women and the family belittles diversity of opinion and the private role of the family.
- Family: Many feel that humans have to live at a much smaller level than society. Feminism of this kind disregards the family (see Chapter 8, pages 169–171).

4 Naturalist/radical feminisms

KEY ISSUE

- What are the moral implications for women if they are fundamentally different from men?

Whereas other forms of feminism have sought either to ignore the body by emphasising reason (liberal feminism) or to consider the public social roles of men and women in a liberated society (social reconstruction feminism), naturalist/radical feminism argues that neither of these two forms of feminism have really considered what it means to be a woman. Naturalist/radical feminism tackles the immensely complex relationship between gender and biology. It is an area fraught with difficulties. Susan Parsons comments:

> The appropriation of a naturalist paradigm of morality is one of the most highly charged and controversial issues within feminist thought.
>
> S Parsons *Feminism and Christian Ethics* (1996) p123

There is no one kind of naturalist feminism. What they all have in common, however, is the radical view that because a woman's body is distinct from the male, her existence can only be ultimately complete when she lives as a woman and not in man's image of a woman. But, as Parsons suggests in the quotation above, how can we define what is 'natural' and how can we know what characteristics are uniquely female?

Philosophically the naturalist feminist is quite different from the liberal feminist. Whereas the liberal wishes to be quite clear that moral values cannot be derived from biology or nature (what is termed the naturalistic fallacy), the naturalist feminist on the other hand feels that it is from her biologically unique status that women's values can and must be derived.

This is hardly new and marks a return to the ancient natural law notion that what is natural is good, and if it is good then there is a duty to make sure that it achieves its full potential. This has its roots in the philosophy of **Aristotle (384–322 BCE)** who considered that all biological processes worked to an 'end' or *telos*. Human rationality is more creative than other animals and allows each person to be actively involved in the process. When this is successful then there is true happiness (*eudomonia*).

a) Reproduction and motherhood

Is being a mother ultimately the *telos* or purpose of being a woman or is this simply a social idea imposed by men? Radical feminists assert both. One group considers modern reproductive technologies to be the great liberator from biological processes while the other group argues that the ability of women to reproduce and rear a child is a unique experience which gives them the power to distinguish themselves from men. Both groups agree that the basis for women's oppression has been the male's power and control over the process of reproduction. This argument clearly follows on from the Marxist model, but whereas for Marx and Engels social history was determined by class struggle between the property-owning classes and the workers, radical feminists argue that the process of history should be understood as the sexual oppression of men over women and the struggle for women to be liberated from sexual slavery.

i Reproduction as liberation

For writers such as **Mary O'Brien** (*The Politics of Reproduction* 1981) reproduction and motherhood give women their unique ability to assert their own identity. Using the Marxist model of insiders and outsiders men are essential outside the reproductive process; only a woman is fully able to own the means of reproduction from conception to birth. However, what has happened in the past is that alienated men have tried to reassert their role in the process and determine when and how women should give birth. For many feminists, whereas contraception allows a woman to choose when to reproduce, other forms of artificial reproduction such as surrogacy and artificial insemination by donor (see Chapter 7) are treated with great caution. All aided forms of reproduction allow men to control a woman's means of reproduction and reduce her to the level of a breeder or prostitute.

ii Reproduction as oppression

However, for many feminists the opportunity offered by reproductive technologies provides the means by which to liberate themselves from the constraints of being a reproducer. **Shulamith Firestone** (*The Dialectic of Sex* 1970) is perhaps one of the more outspoken representatives of this line of thought. In her utopia the dimination of reproduction means that women will no longer be defined by their biology and can enter into the public realm as coequals with men in an **androgynous** society. In the first phase of this revolution women must ensure that they own all the processes of reproduction – abortion, contraception, artificial insemination by donor and so on, for each of these represent a means by which liberation from reproduction will be possible. Ultimately technology will make it possible for a woman to be completely free from all the biological aspects of reproduction.

iii Motherhood as a cultural phenomenon

Is a woman unfulfilled if she does not want to have and to rear children? This strikes at the heart of the radical feminist view that 'motherhood' is the ultimate patriarchal gender construction by men in order to control women. A woman who does not have maternal feelings is considered to be unfeminine.

Ann Oakley presents the view that motherhood is a socially contrived phenomenon and quite separate from being a biological mother. There are three myths or fallacies of motherhood:

all women need to be a mother
all mothers need their children
all children need their mothers

A Oakley *Woman's Work: The Housewife, Past and Present* (1972) p186

Each of these claims can be countered by observation from other cultures and scientific research. Girls from an early age are brought up to play the role of mother – protecting, nurturing and feeding in play with dolls or in the roles assigned for them in the household. 'Maternal instinct' simply does not exist. Many new mothers have no idea how to feed or dress a baby. The most oppressive fallacy is that children need their biological mother more than their father. Oakley argues that children who have been adopted are no less successful than children who have been reared by their biological parents, and that one-to-one parenting has no particular advantage over those children who have been brought up in communes (such as a kibbutz for example). Other feminists suggest a psychological interpretation of 'motherhood' as a woman's means of compensating for her lack of usefulness in the workplace and justifying her role at home. All these attitudes are created by living in a patriarchal society.

However, not all radical feminists take such a hard line as these. Instead they suggest that oppression lies in fulfilling the male expectation of motherhood – real men do not feed, wash, nurture and 'mother' their children. Liberation comes when children are reared not to associate 'motherhood' just with the woman but with both partners. There is even a sense that because feminist values are broader than male ones a child brought up with these will have a greater and richer range of human experiences without the false gender stereotypes inherent in traditional patriarchal families.

b) Sexuality and separation

Most forms of feminism we have looked at so far have sought either to place women on the same economic and political level as men, or to look for a radical transformation of both men and women's gender roles in society. The most radical form of feminism considers that because women's nature is so different from men's, the only whole and ultimately worthwhile life is to be separate from men.

i Rejection of androgyny

Perhaps the most influential and certainly one of the most outspoken writers of this kind of feminism is **Mary Daly**. Her books mark a progression of thought from the acceptance of androgyny to its complete rejection. Her influence though is particularly important because of her Roman Catholic background and her analysis of the Church and its doctrines (see also Post-Christian Feminism pages 38–39).

The inspiration for her naturalism is not Aristotilian but the philosophical visionary Friederich Nietzsche (1844–1900).

Nietzsche's importance for Daly (and other feminists) is that he offers a radical transformation of society in which all the values which had been locked away and guarded by church and institution would be available to humans. But the values which are offered are based on a new understanding of what it means to be human; without God it is humans who have to be creative, powerful, energetic, imaginative. The '**will to power**', as Nietzsche termed this humanistic ethic, cannot be bolted on to existing moralities. It is an uncompromising vision. The 'transformation of values' means that hitherto negative values of pride, competition, lust and greed must replace the old 'slave' mentality of love, forgiveness and tolerance. But this is not a straight swap. To come of age in this new era means that humans must be gloriously self-sufficient and shake off their chains of servitude of all existing institutions and religion.

From Nietzsche Daly draws her inspiration for a radical transformation of a patriarchal society. The old order of male patriarchal values cannot be used as a basis because such values will always taint and distort the new.

● **God:** Nietzsche famously pronounced that 'God is dead'; this is hugely significant for it means that humans are no longer subservient to God as his objects, but are liberated to become their own subjects.
● **Homosexuality:** feminists are not homosexuals, because homosexuality incorporates male patriarchal values.
● **Androgyny:** must now be rejected. Feminism cannot bolt on to the male world, nor can it hope to produce a new male-female product. In both cases male patriarchal values of the old order will distort the new.

So, Nietzsche's 'will to power' is also the radical feminist creed. In male or old order terms, it was understood to be the 'will over' others, but for Daly and others, it means the inner and outer liberation of women as women. As an illustration of what this means, Daly constantly redefines language in its radically non-patriarchal meaning. For instance 'lust' – the title of one of her books, *Pure Lust* (1984) – in its male usage refers to manipulative, self-gratifying exploitative sex whereas in its female liberated sense it refers to the vigorous, lusty and powerful woman.

ii Separation and lesbianism

It does not follow that all lesbians are necessarily feminists, but in the view of Daly and others in order to realise the new feminist vision free from patriarchal influence, the only satisfactory non-exploitative sexual relationship has to be with other women.

Lesbianism is also a public political gesture. It suggests a public rejection of traditional values and a radically new model of human sexuality that does not involve reproduction, motherhood or submission. It is not just symbolic that there is no penetration by the male of the female in sexual intercourse, for all male sex is about domination (feminists often point out how rape, child molesting and sexual abuse are usually performed by men and rarely by women) whilst lesbianism offers women a wholly different kind of sexual relationship as a meeting of sexual equals.

c) Criticisms of naturalist/radical feminisms

i Feminine values fallacy
Radical feminists talk as if it is possible to discern unique, fixed feminist values independent of male patriarchal ones. This supposes firstly, that it is possible to be sufficiently removed from the male view, and their 'false consciousness', to see beyond. Secondly, that these values are in themselves only derived from women. Thirdly, that they are necessarily better or preferable or 'good'. Finally, if these values are in opposition to prevailing social (male) values then as society changes so will women's values.

ii Essentialism
If women's gender role has been shaped by society, then it is equally true that men's genders have been socialised. So, if women seek to be liberated from their perceived gender type then the same is true for men. It does not follow that all men are naturally or essentially potential rapists. Radical feminists have therefore to be consistent and allow that men, just as much as women, can alter their 'false consciousness' and gender perception.

iii Fragmentation and introversion
The formation of women's groups may give women welcome support and encouragement, but their radical stance often alienates other women and the sympathy of men. Furthermore, by rejecting men, some radical feminists behave in just the same way as the men who treat women as inferior. It is difficult to see how this form of feminism is morally superior to the sexist system it has castigated.

5 Christian feminist theology

> **KEY ISSUE**
> ● Can Christian theology fully incorporate contemporary feminism?

Christianity has always assimilated and adjusted to its cultural and philosophical environment and the various feminisms outlined above have all been instrumental in the formation of Christian feminist theology. The insights of secular feminism have enabled Christian theology and ethics to explore new areas and rediscover ideas, which over the centuries, have become obscured or forgotten. But for others the challenge of radical feminism in particular has posed such profound problems that Christianity has been unable to meet the demands of its feminist experience. These so-called **post-Christian feminists** still draw from the Christian tradition but no longer believe in its central claims.

a) Biblical feminist theology

There is sometimes a tendency to treat the Bible as if it were all written by the same person and to treat contradictory passages as evidence of muddled thinking. Biblical theologians today encourage readers to see the text as a narrative responding not only to the events they relate, but to the wider story of God's involvement with people. Stories can be read to interpret each other either by reinforcing an idea or by contrast. There are indeed passages which might be considered sexist, patriarchal and anti-feminist, but as Mary Wollstonecraft commented (page 5), they must be seen as poetical products of the times and circumstances in which they were composed.

i New social order

In the New Testament it is the four gospels which refer most explicitly to the words and teachings of Jesus. It is often pointed out that Jesus' portrayal in these texts presents a far more radical view of men and women than elsewhere in the New Testament. We should be careful here not to make too sharp a contrast. The gospels themselves were written to present Jesus to different communities and although there is a higher historical content than in Paul's letters, they are, nevertheless, theological documents. Jesus was not a feminist; there is no evidence that he had either the philosophical or psychological aims which characterise any of the feminist movements today. But the gospels consistently suggest that his view of women and men challenged many of the deeply ingrained traditions of the time.

His central idea of the Kingdom of God (a new social order based on an intimate personal relationship with God) time and again is shown not to distinguish between rich and poor, outcast and conformist, men and women. The following are only a few examples from many:

● It is the faith of John the Baptist's mother Elizabeth and obedience of Jesus' mother Mary (Luke 1:5–7; 26–38) which permits them to become instruments of God's incarnation in Jesus. It is women who accompany Jesus to the cross, when almost all his male followers have deserted him (Luke 23:27–31), and who are the very first to experience the resurrection (Luke 24:1–11).

● Matthew's genealogy (Matthew 1:1–16) sets out Jesus' forbears and is at pains to link him with a series of women in the Old Testament, not only unusual in itself (as it would be normal only to look at male lineage), but more so because they had been involved with some sexual irregularity. So, the preparation for the coming of the Kingdom of God is a challenge to ancient prejudices against women.

● Whereas traditionally in Judaism a woman could not become a disciple of a rabbi Jesus had many women followers – even when these women were considered social outcasts (Luke 7:36–50; 8:1–3). For this reason Luke uses the story of Mary and Martha (Luke 10:38–42) as a challenge to those who considered a woman's duty to be the carrying out of domestic chores.

ii Purity and women's bodies

Many modern feminist theories account for male aggression towards women as fear of women's bodies. Fear of a woman's sexuality as the seducer is illustrated in the wisdom literature (Proverbs 6:24), or her power of reproduction depicted as a punishment in Genesis 3:16. The Book of Leviticus (15:19–24) refers to the woman's monthly period as a time when she became ritually outcast from the community. Judaism's religious, moral and national identity was defined through purity laws. William Countryman (*Dirt, Greed and Sex* 1988) argues that the early Christian challenge to so many of these taboos including a radical reappraisal of men and women was a way in which it eventually defined its own separate identity.

A highly significant passage occurs in Mark 5:25–34 where Jesus touches a woman who has had internal bleeding for 12 years. His deliberate action dismisses the taboo of touching a woman in public and at the same time rejects the Levitical law which made her an outcast because of her prolonged bleeding. Jesus' own empathy for the woman as a person is described as 'power going out of him'; she is cured not because she is a woman but because of her faith and desire to seek a whole life.

The question of purity rules caused considerable controversy amongst the early Christians. The Council at Jerusalem (Acts 15) debated the question of Gentile admission and whether circumcision was a prerequisite for entry. In these early days Peter learnt that just as the ancient food laws (Acts 10:9–16) were no longer applicable, so also 'God shows no partiality, but in every nation any one who fears him and does what is right is acceptable to him' (Acts 10:34–35). The utterly consistent view held by the very early church was that **baptism** marked a new moment in the life of the convert. Paul, who understood this as the essence of the Christian gospel, concluded in one train of thought in his letter to the Galatians (having justified his rejection of purity rules of circumcision and table fellowship):

> For as many of you as were baptised into Christ have put on Christ. There is neither Jew nor Greek, there is neither slave nor free, there is neither male nor female; for you are all one in Christ Jesus.

> Galatians 3:27-28

There are many implications for Christian feminists today. Purity might imply any circumstance where a women is debarred from a job or employment for no other reason than her sexuality. But overcoming purity taboos also suggests that at a fundamental level, deep seated prejudices about women's sexual inferiority, will need a change in male consciousness.

iii Women's roles

The biggest challenge for the feminist biblical theologian is the interpretation of passages which do not fit into the emerging pattern that 'in Christ there is neither male nor female'. It is often considered that Paul appears to be at very least inconsistent with himself. In 1 Corinthians 14:34–36 Paul forbids women to speak in Church and stipulates that they should seek to be educated by their husbands at home, a view also reiterated by the author of 1 Timothy (probably a follower of Paul):

> 1 Let a woman learn silence with all submissiveness. I permit no woman to teach or have authority over men; she is to keep silent. For Adam was formed first, then Eve; and Adam was not deceived, but the woman was deceived and became a transgressor. Yet woman will be saved
> 5 through bearing children, if she continues in faith and love and holiness, with modesty.

> 1 Timothy 2:11–15

To these can be added the 'household rules' – lists of duties for men, women and children, found in 1 Timothy 3:1–13 and 1 Peter 2:11–3:12.

> Likewise you wives, be submissive to your husbands, so that some, though they do not obey the word, may be won without a word by the behaviour of their wives, when they see your chaste and reverent behaviour.

> 1 Peter 3:1–2

But for the liberal feminist theologian, the passage illustrates just how difficult it was for some early Christian communities to implement the radical social demands of the gospel. For why reprimand the women in the community unless women were already practising their new found freedom and causing some embarrassment with Jews and Gentiles. The author of 1 Peter says as much:

> Maintain good conduct among the Gentiles, so that in case they speak against you as wrongdoers, they may see your good deeds.

> 1 Peter 2:12

Finally, Paul explicitly mentions the assistance of women among his co-workers, Priscilla (Acts 18:1,18,26), Apphia (Philemon 2) and Phoebe (Romans 16:1–2).

b) Feminism and women's ministry

1   On another occasion I was led in the imagination down to the sea-bed, and there I saw green hills and valleys looking as though they were moss-covered, with seaweed and sand. This I understood to mean that if a man or woman were under-sea and saw God ever present with him
5   (as indeed God is) he would be safe in body and soul, and take no hurt. Moreover he would know comfort and consolation beyond all power to tell. For God's will is that by faith we should see him continuously, though it seems to us that we are seeing him so little. By this faith he makes us ever to gain grace. His will is to be seen; his will is to be
10 sought; his will is to be awaited and trusted.

> Mother Julian of Norwich *Revelations of Divine Love* Chapter 10

The debate about women's ministry in the Church is as old as Christianity itself. As we have seen it was a live issue in New Testament times and has continued to be so up to the present day. The significance of the debate is far more than whether women can have a public place in the Church (i.e. in the running of church services). It raises fundamental questions about the Christian understanding of a woman's relationship with God in creation and redemption, two issues which have important implications for all aspects of Christian theology.

The quotation above from **Mother Julian of Norwich** (*c*1342–*c*1413) is just one of many which illustrate how a woman's experience of God, as depth and intimacy, expresses a dimension of God which validates the need for male and female ministry. But the experience of 'God as She', is far older than this and, as feminist theologians often demonstrate, persistently appears in ancient Judaism and Christianity (see Ruether *Sexism and God-Talk* Chapter 2).

i Arguments against women's ministry
● Only a man can represent Jesus at the Holy Communion
● Jesus appointed men as apostles – and commissioned Peter as the foundation of the Church (Matthew 16:18–19)

- Conservative Christians (see below page 40) argue that it is simply not in the God-given order of things for a woman to speak or teach in public. Man was created before woman (1 Timothy 2:11–13).
- Because the man is publicly the 'head of the woman' (Ephesians 5:23) a woman's role is home-maker not minister.

ii Women's ministry as a symbol of equality
For liberal feminists (see pages 20–23 above) the establishment of women ministers is a natural stage in the process of equality and a recovery of Christianity's earliest notion that 'in Christ there is neither male nor female' (Galatians 3:27–28) and that all Christians are 'a royal priesthood' (1 Peter 2:9). Christians have frequently from the earliest days quoted these texts to justify women's ministry.

iii Women's ministry as social reconstruction
Feminist theologians who use the social reconstructionist feminist model view the Kingdom of God to be much more than simply a question of equality between the sexes (see pages 23–27 above). The promise of the Holy Spirit expresses radical challenge to *all* existing social conditions for men and women. The significance of the Spirit (the female aspect of God) symbolises the redemption of the world as a new act of creation. For the author of Acts of the Apostles, at least, the Kingdom of God is a reality now. The Spirit reverses the Fall of Adam and Eve (Genesis 3), and recreates the original relationship between man and woman in creation.

> I will pour out my Spirit upon all flesh, and your sons and your daughters shall prophesy… and on my menservants and my maidservants in those days I will pour out my Spirit; and they shall prophesy.
>
> Acts 2:17–18 see also Joel 2:28–32

There are some important implications for the Church here, just as there are for secular society. Should a church of men and women's ministry maintain its present hierarchical (and patriarchal) structure of laity-priests-bishops? If women are to function fully in the ministry of the church then the language of worship and prayer must be re-written to accommodate an inclusive female-male Christian experience. Against this has to be weighed the importance of continuity with the past and the fear of splitting apart traditionalists and progressives.

iv Women's ministry as radical alternative
But for many feminist theologians the liberal and the reconstructivist fail to address women as distinct from men. The criticisms are similar to those (see pages 23 and 27) of the secular feminist. The tendency is either towards androgyny or inclusivism neither of which account for the *difference* between men and women. Rosemary Radford

Ruether (*Sexism and God-Talk* 1983) argues that the natural/radical feminist theologian poses three possibilities:

● Women's ministry holds the key to the lost self by transforming male values into female values.
● Women's ministry would simply be different and complement the ministry of men.
● Women's ministry is so radically different from men that it would entail separating themselves entirely from any existing church.

So it is unclear whether women can have a role as ministers in the church. The first possibility would only work if men were willing to accept radical change and the third possibility appears either to extend the ancient idea of separate communities for women not as nunneries (which are dependent on men to conduct the mass or holy communion) but religious communities independent of men. An example might be the **Women-Church** which was founded in 1983 after a conference in Chicago. It has no permanent leadership or central organisation but is composed of local base communities in affiliation with one another. For many women it provides the spiritual resource for them to continue within their existing traditions whilst giving them the support to transform them.

c) Post-Christian feminisms

> It might be interesting to speculate upon the probable length of a 'depatriarchalised Bible'. Perhaps there would be enough salvageable material to comprise an interesting pamphlet.
>
> M Daly *Beyond God the Father* (1973) p205

Can Christianity accommodate feminism and survive? This chapter has already suggested that radical feminism not only poses fundamental challenges to politics, economics and philosophy but to religion. Those who are described as post-Christian feminists fall broadly into two kinds.

i Mary Daly: death of God
The first kind begins with a Christian world view but find it utterly incompatible with feminism. Mary Daly is an influential example of one who uses Christian ideas but inverts them: God becomes the symbol of the empowered woman, just as Nietzsche replaced a dead God with a new reinvigorated human, the 'superman' (see pages 31–32 above).

ii Daphne Hampson: non-patriarchal spirituality
The second kind of post-Christian feminists, such as Daphne Hampson (*After Christianity* 1996) are those who still find some

resonance in Christian spirituality but discover that its central theological claims are irredeemably androcentric and patriarchal. But because radical feminism rejects the narrowness of enlightenment rationality, the traditional objections to religion have lost their finality. Radical post-Christian feminism observes all that is wrong with Christianity and offers its own woman-centred spirituality.

● **Dualism:** Christianity depicts God as an objective, self-existing, 'father'. Even expressing God as mother or Goddess fails to alter the master/slave relationship between God, the subject (creator and 'male'), and the world, the object ('other' and 'female').
● **Otherness:** Women in Christian thought will always be the 'other', the object of men. Mary epitomises the one who is submissive and the object of God.
● **Love:** Whole relationships, in women's experience, are formed through equal, reciprocated love. This is what the notion of 'god' represents. There must be no object–subject relationship as there is in so much of Christian theology.

Hampson is impressed by the Christian vision of God who liberates men and women from oppression, in a gender free existence in Christ 'in whom there is neither male nor female' and who epitomises love (1 John 4:16). But as long as God is considered as one who acts 'over' humans, all human relationships will inevitably be destroyed by the slave mentality which is inherent in patriarchal monotheism.

d) Conservative anti-feminist theology

The Right believes that the only way to have a relationship with God is through gender; in doing so, it dismisses concerns about material oppression and reinterprets women's role as mother and housewife as natural fulfilling, even liberating…. many forms of feminism – both secular and Christian – valorize only those women who go to work.

K Rudy *Sex and the Church* (1997) p43

The view expressed here by Kathy Rudy (*Sex and the Church*, 1997) could well summarise the arguments of the radical feminists (see page 25) who have campaigned for wages for housework and the acknowledgement that a woman's role in the house is as valid as a man's external role in the workplace. However, although they may share this superficial aim the 'Right', which Rudy refers to here, are the powerful Christian conservatives whose influence in the United States of America has had a profound effect on middle-class morality and politics.

The rise of right-wing conservative Christianity has its roots in the fundamentalist evangelical movements associated with the Pentecostal churches and southern Baptist churches earlier this century, but as Rudy argues, the movement today cuts across all major denominations. A key driving force of such groups as the Moral Majority, the National Christian Action Coalition, the Religious Round Table and the Christian Voice, is a mistrust of all liberal ideologies and in particular feminism. Liberalism and feminism in both secular and Christian forms are, they argue, the principal reason for increased divorce, dysfunctional families and sexual immorality (in particular homosexuality) corrupting the morals of the young and ultimately undermining the American social dream of a happy prosperous nation.

i Gendered theology

Conservative theology believes that men and women were created differently by God, not to be unequal but to have quite different roles contingent on their gender. This notion is grounded in the creation itself:

> So God created man in his own image, in the image of God he created him; male and female he created them.
>
> Genesis 1:27

But for the conservative the image of God is only accomplished when men and women complete the roles assigned to them. In Genesis this is stated after the fall as being:

1   To the woman he said, 'I will greatly multiply your pain in childbearing; in pain you shall bring forth children, yet your desire shall be for your husband, and he shall rule over you.' And to Adam he said, 'Because you have listened to the voice of your wife, and have eaten of the tree of
5   which I commanded you, 'You shall not eat of it,' cursed is the ground because of you; in toil you shall eat of it all the days of your life; thorns and thistles it shall bring forth to you; and you shall eat the plants of the field. In the sweat of your face you shall eat bread till you return to the ground, for out of it you were taken; you are dust, and to dust you
10 shall return.' The man called his wife's name Eve, because she was the mother of all living.

> Genesis 3:16–20

A woman's role is to be wife and mother and create the 'domestic haven' to which her husband can escape from the external world. But submissiveness is not equated with weakness, after all Eve is depicted as the 'mother of the living' and a mother's role is one who brings life into the world, nurtures it and educates it into the knowledge and love of God. Conservative theology is especially critical of those who confuse these roles. A woman who works outside the home not only removes a job from a man, but diminishes a man's role and his responsibilities to his wife. Those who are persuaded by feminism are not liberated but exploited (see page 23 above for the problems faced by liberal feminism).

ii Dualism and complementarity

One of the strengths of Christian conservatism is its strong sense of right and wrong. Whereas liberalism by its very nature is based on tolerance, individuality, diversity and moral pluralism, conservatism is united by its sense that moral wrongs are sinful, external and belong to the world of evil. The effectiveness of the Right in the USA is due to its powerful and single-minded evangelism through television and politics against what it sees as social evil. This dualism or 'two-ness' extends to the family and society: the family is where Christian piety, love and salvation are developed, the world (where men work) is potentially evil until transformed by the family. Thus men and women have a dual and complementary role in the evangelizing of society. The woman provides the spiritual basis for the family, whilst the husband provides for it materially (see Chapter 8 page 165).

iii Salvation

It follows then that salvation is only fully possible in a heterosexual married Christian relationship. Marriage re-establishes the original covenant between God and man made at the creation. The single life, cohabitation and homosexual relationships all (to different extents) fall short. A woman's role in the process of salvation is particularly significant. Her relationship to God the Father mirrors her complementary role with her husband. The 'maleness' of God is essential in order for the woman to have her own identity and purpose. Seeing God as Father, rather than being a barrier as many feminist Christians argue, on the contrary validates a woman's unique sexual value. To think of 'God as She' makes a woman's own special spiritual role quite redundant. Finally, the woman's role as the submissive, patient and self-sacrificing partner directly correlates with the person of Jesus, whose own sacrificial death redeems and overcomes human sin.

In theory, therefore, a woman's spiritual role ought to enable her to have a unique vocation as a minister or priest – and in some cases such as Phoebe Palmer (Methodist preacher) or Catherine Booth (the founder of the Salvation Army) this has been so. In practice, the biblical texts which forbid a woman to teach in public (1 Timothy 2:11ff, see page 35 above) have been observed by the fundamentalist wing as a direct command by God. Other conservatives have applied the criterion that women's ministry has infringed on the public role of their husbands in the external world. Maybe it has just come too close to the liberal Christian and feminist arguments supporting women leaders or ministers.

Answering structured and essay questions

Use the following diagram as a basis for your summary notes. Add ideas which are shared by the different feminist traditions and indicate how these have affected Christian theology.

Summary diagram

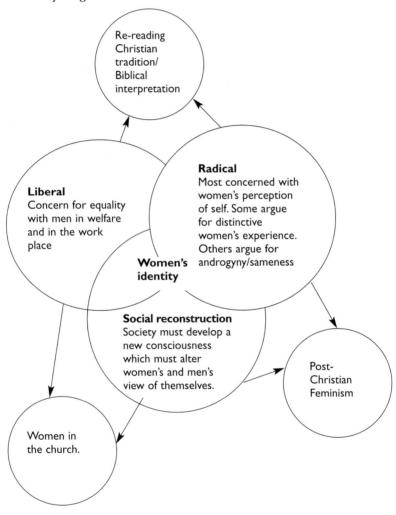

Questions

1. **a)** Explain what is meant by sexism?
    b) Discuss which type of feminist best tackles sexism best today.
2. **a)** Explain why there is more than one kind of feminism.
    b) Assess how effectively theologians have responded to modern feminism.
3. Has feminism done society more harm than good? Discuss
4. Assess the view that Christianity is fundamentally sexist and patriarchal.
5. Does women's liberation mean being free from men? Discuss

Essay skills

Feminism is a vast topic and you will have to be selective. Show that you know that there are many kinds of feminism and that they are determined by very different views of biology, philosophy, psychology, sociology and theology. Try not to limit feminism merely to questions of equality at work (even though this is important) but consider how it challenges the way men understand themselves, how it challenges the way society orders itself. Secular feminisms have also fundamentally affected the way in which scholars have understood history, literature, art and so on. The challenge for theology, and Christian theology in particular, can also be in terms of history (how has Christianity viewed women and men from the early days to the present) and literature (the writings of women and portrayal of women in the Bible). However, an essay such as question 4 above questions the very foundations of theology. Your response might be that certain kinds of feminisms are flawed, or that the notion of God is not a form of repression but liberation, or that the challenge is not from feminism to Christianity, but the other way round.

4 Homosexuality: sexual liberty and consent

1 Homosexual politics

1   Oscar Wilde and Alfred Taylor, the crime of which you have been convicted is so bad that one has to put stern restraint upon one's self to prevent one's self from describing it, in language which I would rather not use, the sentiments which must rise to the breast of every
5   man of honour who has heard the details of these two terrible trials… People who can do these things must be dead to all sense of shame, and one cannot hope to produce any effect upon them. It is the worse case I have ever tried. That you, Taylor kept a kind of male brothel it is impossible to doubt. And that you, Wilde, have been the centre of a

10   circle of extensive corruption of the most hideous kind among young
     men, it is equally impossible to doubt... The sentence of the Court is
     that each of you be imprisoned and kept to hard labour for two years.

Mr Justice Wills summing up at the trial of Oscar Wilde, 1895

1   If we go down the path of treating one group of members of society
     in a different way from another, it has to be based upon grounds and
     criteria which should be capable of public justification. This would seem
     to me in the present context to imply that such discrimination could
5   be justified for three main reasons, if those reasons were valid – which
     I do not believe they are. The first is that homosexuality is morally
     wrong and therefore should not yield the same rights as heterosexual
     relations. The second is that such relations can cause harm to the
10   individual who seeks to exercise the rights which the Bill would confer.
     The third is that extending those rights would cause harm to others. I
     do not believe that any of those claims can be sustained.

Lord Plant of Highfield, 13 April 1999
Debate in the House of Lords on the Sexual Offences (Amendment) Bill
in Parliamentary Debates Vol 599 No 64 column 697

These two public statements mark not only the start of the
homosexuality debate and the nature of the present political
controversy but also the range of moral and philosophical issues
which homosexuality poses. A great deal has changed since Mr Justice
Wills summed up at Oscar Wilde's famous trial and Lord Plant's
contribution to the Lords' debate whether the age of consent should
be the same for homosexual men as heterosexuals (i.e. 16 instead of
18 years of age).

In 1895 the term 'homosexual' had only just been invented and
society took its lead in most matters from Christian moral principles.
One hundred years later, following the influence of women's
movements, the liberalising of people's attitudes to sex and the
diminishing influence of a Christian-based single morality,
homosexuality has emerged as a distinctively 'gay lifestyle'.

Homosexuality is a political as well as a moral issue but the social
questions it raises are broader than homosexuality itself.

● Should laws permit people to behave in a way which others regard as
  morally repellent?
● Does homosexuality threaten or harm the moral stability of society?
● Is sexual lifestyle an entirely private affair?
● Is the debate about homosexuality purely a rights issue? Should laws
  which discriminate against homosexuals be changed?
● How far should the Church tolerate or change its views to
  accommodate shifting social views of human sexual behaviour?

a) Gay, lesbian or queer?

The English term **homosexuality** was invented in 1892 to translate the German word used by psychologists to describe what they understood to be a 'pathology' or psychological imbalance (or sexual 'inversion' as it was termed). In the minds of many, homosexuality still represents a distorted or deviant form of sexual relationship. Many prefer the term **gay** to describe same-sex male relationships to indicate that this form of lifestyle is far from being seedy, clandestine and oppressive (as it is often regarded by its critics) but happy and liberating.

Some favour the use of **queer** (originally a term of abuse) to include many forms of sexual lifestyle which are rejected by traditional society because, almost by definition, its sexual nonconformity challenges society to widen its understanding of what it means to have a full human relationship outside the stereotype of the heterosexual (man/woman) norm.

In most literature it is usual to use the term homosexual to refer to all self-consciously chosen same-sex sexual relationships. We must be careful here to distinguish same-sex relationships which however intense, are not sexual but are on the level of friendship. Women argue that their relationships are very different to male–male relations: it is customary now to use the term **lesbian** as a means of distinguishing female homosexuality from male homosexuality. So, homosexuality is generally taken to mean both lesbian and gay relationships. Some prefer the use of **same-sex relationships** so as to avoid the negative connotations sometimes associated with homosexuality and because it also includes **bisexuality** where heterosexual men and women also have sexual relationships with people of their own sex.

b) Nature or nurture

There is no conclusive evidence whether a person is born homosexual or whether it is the result of upbringing induced by childhood trauma or whether it is a lifestyle choice. However, whereas there is broad agreement as to what biologically constitutes a man or a woman there is fundamental disagreement whether homosexuality is even part of the nature or nurture discussion. Nevertheless there is a political as well as a personal interest in knowing the **aetiology** (or origins) of why a certain minority of people consider that they are homosexual.

i Nature: the gay gene

The quest for the so-called 'gay gene' was pioneered by Dean Hamer, a molecular geneticist in 1991. What he discovered was a sex-linked connection on one arm of the X chromosome inherited by males from their mothers. Although he did not find a gay gene itself, as he admits, 'we only detected its presence through linkage'. He went on to say:

> 1 More precisely our mapping showed the 'gay gene' is most likely somewhere between markers GABRA$_3$ and DXYS$_{154}$, which span a distance of about five million base pairs. That represents less than 0.2 of the three billion base pairs in the human genome, but because the
> 5 genome includes somewhere around 100,000 genes, such a small area has enough room for up to 200 or so different genes. Narrowing a search to two hundred apartments in a big city isn't very helpful if you are looking for one person.

D Hamer and P Copeland *The Science of Desire*
quoted in R Nye *Sexuality* (1999) p289

Hamer's argument, along with all those who consider that 'it is all in the genes', assumes that a person's character can be determined by **reductionism**, or a complete knowledge of their physical make-up. Reductionism at the very best might suggest a possible character potential, but can a single gene or even a collection of genes determine whether a person is honourable or light-hearted or avaricious? By his own admission Hamer concludes that his present research can only locate a cluster or 'linkage' of genes. This suggests that sexuality is not something that can be pinned down to something as definite as a gene. It is just as likely that there are other social factors as well.

ii Nurture: socialisation

A radical and controversial alternative to the biological and psychological search for the homosexual nature is suggested by the influential French philosopher **Michel Foucault (1926–1984)**. Foucault argues that all attempts to classify human sexuality into normal or abnormal are misplaced and dangerous. He argues that if we look back in history we will see that the idea of sex and gender was far less rigid than has become the case over the past two hundred years. Different cultures at different times judged sexual behaviour in terms of acceptable and non-acceptable practices, but were not interested in trying to classify men's and women's natures into fixed categories (see Chapter 2 page 15).

Part 2 of *The History of Sexuality: The Use of Pleasure* (1984) is particularly important in the discussion of homosexuality. In Part 1 Foucault had distinguished between what he called the *ars erotica* and the *scientia sexualis*. The *ars erotica* he claimed, was a much healthier view of sex in which the individual was constrained in what he did only by his role in society not by his sexual nature. The *scientia sexualis* on the other hand are a peculiarly Western modern phenomenon whereby the discourses of scientists, psychologists and politicians have, in their attempt to define the truth, categorised people according to what is normal and what is abnormal. Homosexuality, or 'inversion' as it was called, was 'produced' in the 19th century, as a mutant category when it failed to meet the definitions of sex established by the biologists, psychologists and politicians.

Thus homosexuality, according to Foucault's argument, has emerged in a curious way. First, the repressive treatment of homosexual practices has been largely politically inspired by the middle classes who have imposed the heterosexual family norm as the most productive economic basis for society. Second, repression has caused homosexuals to invent their own 'reverse discourse' in defence. That is homosexuals have had to create their own identity and practices either by equating it with heterosexuality or more recently by saying how it is different (see above on queer theory). Although Foucault's argument suggests that homosexuality certainly exists and has its own identity, he is not suggesting that there is a homosexual nature – any more than there is a male or female sexual nature. When he was asked whether homosexuality was the result of nature or nurture, Foucault answered, 'On this question I have absolutely nothing to say. "No comment"' (quoted in T Spargo *Foucault and Queer Theory* p83).

Foucault's argument for the emergence of homosexual identity begins with an analysis of Greek culture before Christianity. Whereas many refer to ancient Greek culture as an example of explicit homosexuality, Foucault's reading of the situation is different. The sexual discourse of Ancient Greece concentrated on its practices within a range of other social expectations.

SAME-SEX RELATIONSHIPS IN ANCIENT GREECE

● Erotic love or desire must be understood in the context of a man's concern for his body (its well-being through diet, sleep and exercise), his relationship with his wife (seen largely in economic terms as control of the household) and '*chresis aphrodision*' (Greek for 'the management of pleasure') or self mastery. The final element is not to be confused with modern ideas of ethics. Rather than laying down a specific ethical code, ethics were governed by whatever was considered to be beautiful, moderate, balanced and fulfilling.
● An adult married man could have a sexual relationship with a boy or a girl. It was not considered to be a threat to the economic running of the household or a threat to his wife.
● The object or *telos* of love (Urania heavenly love) for a boy was considered higher than sexual love (for reproduction) for a woman.
● The relationship with a boy (*paidika*) was considered bad if the boy was over an age where he might be considered an adult – his

beauty would have waned, it would cease to be an 'aesthetic' or beautiful expression of erotic love.
- Male prostitutes and boys who were too 'easy' or keen on sex, was often criticised because of the unbalanced nature of the relationship. The male prostitute became the passive partner and eros (love), corrupted by excess desire, became adulterated to a lower pleasure.
- Many philosophers were critical of relationships which exploited the young (see Socrates' first speech in Plato's *Phaedrus*) or which were decadent

Foucault's analysis concludes that unlike the present time the ancient Greeks did not think in terms of a homosexual nature, what is described is essentially bisexuality, but nor or the other hand was there complete freedom to behave in any way one wished – certain forms of 'homosexuality' were regarded with great disgust.

Foucault's theory of seeing human sexual history as a series of discourses suggests two implications for the present debate about homosexuality.

- Firstly, homosexuality in its present form is an important phenomenon of modern Western societies. Its existence challenges all our views of sexuality, social institutions and morality.
- Secondly, if homosexuality does not have a fixed nature, then what form will it take in the future as it develops its own 'discourse'? Could it even disappear?

c) Homosexual difference

For lesbians and gays 'difference' describes the fundamental psychological or even spiritual dimension of same-sex relationships. Perhaps we could consider a gay relationship to be analogous to visiting a different country with a very different culture from our own. Viewed from the outside it might seem to be exotic, frightening, even bizarre, but nevertheless entirely valid from within its own terms of cultural reference (i.e. gay and lesbian orientation and experience).

Like some forms of feminism this entails rejecting many heterosexual values, traditions and social structures. For instance in some countries where homosexual marriage (or 'registered partnership') is possible, radicals consider this 'normalising' of homosexual relationships to be entirely false being based on heterosexual values which are alien to homosexual nature and identity. For lesbian feminists inclusion into patriarchal institutions such as a marriage (see pages 31–32) are a double enslavement to male patriarchy as well as ownership. It is often for this reason that the term 'homosexual' is avoided because the use of 'male' or '*homo*' (in

Latin) implies that a homosexual relationship is really only valid when it mimics a 'proper' male heterosexual one. Thus the closer a homosexual relationship is to the heterosexual norm the less of a threat it is perceived to be and the more it can be included.

But for radicals this entirely misses the point. Elizabeth Stuart, for instance, even criticises the 'pseudo-radical' in the church who argue for the inclusion of lesbians and gays in the running of the church, on the grounds of unconscious **homosexism**:

1   Pseudo-radicals have no interest in non-monogamous, flamboyant, lesbian, gay and bisexual people. The debate about homosexuality in the churches is so stale and repetitious because it is not really about homosexuality. It is about heterosexuality and how far the mantle of

5   heterosexuality can be flung – what are the borders? Certainly, homosexuality triggered the debate, but the discussion of lesbian and gay lives masks what is actually going, namely the assumption and preservation of heterosexual normativity, by inclusion rather than exclusion. This is why it is homophobia – irrational fear of homosexual

10   persons – that is named as the sin in theological discourse and not heterosexism – the assumption of heterosexual superiority. Hence, church leaders can constantly condemn homophobia while supporting or condoning legislation that discriminates against lesbian and gay people and do absolutely nothing about the violence, discrimination

15   and marginalization lesbian and gay people encounter inside and outside the church.

> E Stuart 'Sex in Heaven' in
> J Davies and G Loughlin *Sex These Days* (1998) p187

And if Stuart and others are right, then homosexuality and especially lesbianism when driven by radical feminism, do indeed pose disruptive and fundamental challenges to ethicists, legislators and theologians alike. So, are there legitimate grounds to limit homosexual behaviour?

2 Consenting adults and public morality

KEY ISSUE

● Is society a happier, fairer and more exciting place if all its members are left to choose whatever sexual lifestyle they wish?

Lord Plant's argument quoted at the start of this chapter expresses what is central to the liberal argument established by John Stuart Mill (1806–1873) and applied by the Wolfenden report in its examination of homosexuality and prostitution in 1957. The resulting legislation in the **Sexual Offences Act** (1967) is particularly important because it expresses the difficult relationship between what Mill called **experiments in living** (in this case homosexuality), public morality and the place of the law. The act incorporates Mill's notion of democratic liberty:

● to preserve public order and decency from injury
● to safeguard against exploitation and corruption of others (especially the vulnerable)
● to permit consenting adults to conduct their lives without the interference of the law.

But all these notions beg questions. In the case of Oscar Wilde, for example, the judge, Mr Justice Wills, considered Wilde's behaviour to be a threat, an 'extensive corruption' to public decency. But by what standard can one judge public decency? From the liberal and utilitarian point of view the only clear argument for the curtailment of homosexuality would have to be based on empirical (factual) evidence that it does harm the health of society. But others argue that homosexuality is *a priori* morally wrong and corrupt and the law should uphold the public moral values of society.

a) Consent

Earlier in the 19th century, well before Oscar Wilde's trial, the philosopher and legal reformer **Jeremy Bentham (1748–1832)** had written over three hundred manuscript pages on same-sex relationships unpublished in his lifetime. His aim was to consider whether, according to the **utilitarian** principle ('the greatest good of the greatest number'), anal sex or 'unnatural' acts between men and men, including children, should be considered criminal acts and punishable by death. The first important principle Bentham argues in *Offences Against One's Self: Paederasty* (*c*1785), is that mutual consent for pleasure cannot make pederasty in itself wrong:

1 As to any primary mischief, it is evident that it produces no pain in anyone. On the contrary it produces pleasure, and that a pleasure which, by their perverted taste, is by this supposition preferred to that pleasure which is in general reputed the greatest. The partners are both
5 willing. If either of them be unwilling, the act is not that which we have here in view; it is an offence totally different in its nature of effects; it is personal injury; it is a kind of rape.

quoted in M Blasius and S Phelan *We are Everywhere* (1997) p16

The second is whether it harms society and causes unhappiness. This can be taken either to mean physical harm (it depletes the population, robs women of their roles, it causes illness) or moral harm (it undermines the family and marriage or causes offence).

Bentham argues that those who oppose 'unnatural' sexual acts do so on irrational prejudice or superstition (religion) and not on rational utilitarian principles. Bentham's principle probably strikes many people as being self-evident; providing both parties are in agreement then morally it can do no harm. However, there are difficulties determining whether this notion of **consent as contract** is entirely coherent.

● Consent may fail to take into account long term harmful psychological side-effects.
● Consent is contingent on determining whether a person is capable of making a reasoned decision.
● Consent may be 'apparent consent'. I may consent to lend you my car because you have asked me as a favour. Nevertheless, it is not something I do willingly because I know you are a bad driver.
● Consent distorts other moral considerations. It makes the contract more important than the persons involved; in Christian and Kantian terms contract treats people as means and not ends in themselves.
● Consent is only possible when all things really are equal. Marxism claims that until economic and class distinctions are overcome we all live with a 'false consciousness' of equality.

b) Liberty, equality and rights

Bentham and later John Stuart Mill helped to establish the liberal **positivist** view of law, i.e. that law has emerged from social custom and tradition, but is not in itself a moral authority. It is this view which Lord Plant expressed in the House of Lords. The function of law is therefore to facilitate the maximum liberties of each citizen whilst protecting the liberties of minorities against 'the tyranny of the state'. The question of homosexuality poses an important challenge to the liberal principle of law. Should the law permit homosexual practice on the grounds that what consenting adults do in private should be left to their own moral discretion even if many are morally offended? Bentham argued on utilitarian grounds that prohibition could only increase suspicion and fear. Liberty must be considered publicly in terms of equality and rights.

i Liberty
John Stuart Mill states the liberal principle in this way:

1 The only freedom which deserves the name is that of pursuing our own good in our own way, so long as we do not attempt to deprive others of theirs or impede their efforts to obtain it. Each is proper guardian of his own health, whether bodily or mental and spiritual. Mankind are
5 greater gainers by suffering each other to live as seems good to themselves than by compelling each to live as seems good to the rest.

J S Mill *On Liberty* (1974) p72

Liberty may be defined in two way: **negative liberty**, that is the least interference of the state or anyone else to restrict individual behaviour and **positive liberty**, that is the freedom to act within certain constraints (the law, social custom). Mill's position, expressed in the quotation above, is largely a defence based on negative liberty. Mill supports negative liberty especially when it comes to 'experiments in living' because, in utilitarian terms:

● Variety of lifestyles enhances the richness and enjoyment of society.
● Liberty allows individuals to 'flourish and breathe' according to their own wishes and rational choices.
● Lack of restraint creates imaginative individuals who can contribute positively to society.
● We acknowledge that we are all fallible and make mistakes; no one can have a monopoly on morality.
● Tolerance makes for a happier society.

There are many responses to Mill's notion of liberty and in particular to the case of homosexuality and 'experiments in living':

● Variety does not necessarily make for a happier society. A community working within common values and aims and sense of purpose might feel freer (positive liberty). Profusion of lifestyles may simply lead to confusion, distrust, anxiety and unhappiness.
● Sometimes creative individuals do emerge from oppressive societies. It does not follow that freedom to do as one wishes without constraint makes for a more imaginative society.
● Mill's argument assumes that people do make rational and sensible choices. Often the kind of choices people make are detrimental to themselves and far from creating an environment in which to flourish.

ii Equality

More problematic is whether gay and lesbian men and women should be treated equally under the law. Some argue that if the liberal principle is accepted, then equality and civil liberties should be extended as to any other minority groups. There are two principles which might be applied here: **equality of opportunity**, which takes into account appropriate personal qualities and abilities, and **equality of consideration**, which gives all like interests and skills the same weighting.

The response to these principles is complicated by the claims of some gays and lesbians that because they are different they do not wish to be normalised into heterosexual culture. Thus whilst consideration of opportunity may remove prejudices concerning employment, it is less clear whether under the principle of equality of consideration a homosexual couple wishing to adopt children, marry or be considered a couple, have the appropriate qualities and abilities like a heterosexual couple.

iii Rights

The final element in the liberal model of democracy is the place of rights. Rights serve to protect the individual from exploitation as well as permitting certain basic human liberties. Where existing law does exploit or harm, rights can act as 'trumps' (as Ronald Dworkins calls them) forcing legal reform whether the majority are in favour or not. European gay and lesbian reform groups cite two rights from the European Convention on Human Rights as the basis for their claim that many laws should be revised.

> Everyone has the right to respect for his private and family life, his home and his correspondence.
>
> Article 8

> The enjoyment of the rights and freedoms set forth in this Convention shall be secured without discrimination on any ground such as sex, race, colour, language, religion, political or other opinion, national or social origin, association with a national minority, property, birth or other status.
>
> Article 14

For instance in the United Kingdom the law states that gays and lesbians:

- May not marry.
- Are not treated as a couple for inheritance (under the 1975 Provision for Families and Dependants Act for example) or council housing.
- Do not enjoy the same protection of sex discrimination laws in employment, or benefits to a partner (e.g. cheap travel, health insurance, pensions,etc).
- May not jointly adopt a child. Where adoption is granted only one of the couple becomes the legal parent.
- May not have sex until 18, unlike heterosexual couples who may have sex at 16 (the age of consent).

Gay and lesbian pressure groups such as **Stonewall** cite many cases where homosexuals are discriminated against in the workplace simply because they are homosexual. Whereas the law outlaws heterosexual sexism, it does not yet extend this to all forms of sexual orientation. If the **Sex Discrimination Act** (1975) were to be amended would organisations who disapprove of homosexuality be forced to change? Would it, for instance, be illegal for a Christian boarding school for boys to turn down a well-qualified teacher if it was discovered he was gay? Fear of sexual harassment as a form of harm certainly has less weight now that women in many armed forces train and fight alongside men.

In many European countries the recognition that homosexual relationships are valid and should have the similar protection of the law as heterosexual marriages has already taken place. **Registered partnerships,** as they are often termed, have become law in Denmark (1989), Sweden (1995), Iceland (1996), Greenland (1996) and the Netherlands (1997). Partnerships are different from marriages only in so far as they exclude the right to joint adoption of children (although Dutch law permits the adoption of Dutch children), may only occur when one of the partners is a citizen of that country (whereas marriage is legally recognised by any country in the world) and are only recognised in that country.

There have already been some important challenges and changes to the law. But the Convention is sensitive to the traditions of a country. For instance article 12 states that:

> Men and women of marriageable age have the right to marry and to found a family, according to the national laws governing the exercise of this right.

There is no automatic right to gay and lesbian marriage in Britain according to 'national laws', but with the passing of the **Human Rights** Act (1998) the European Convention is already being employed by pressure groups to challenge many traditional aspects of life.

c) Moral harm

KEY ISSUE

● Can the law appeal in difficult cases to a public sense of what is right and wrong?

The third element of Mill's liberty principle which was adopted by the Wolfenden report in its decriminalising of homosexuality, is whether lifestyle choices or 'experiments in living' should be limited because they cause harm. It is easy to see from a utilitarian point of view that if harm is caused to society then overall happiness will be reduced and the law has a legitimate right to intervene. But happiness, just as much as harm, is an ambiguous notion and hard to define and judge.

i Personal harm
Mill states clearly that self-harm is one's own affair:

> The only purpose for which power can be rightfully exercised over any member of a civilised community, against his own will, is to prevent harm to others. His own good, either physical or moral, is not a sufficient warrant.

J S Mill *On Liberty* (1974) p68

The argument here makes an important distinction between **necessary and sufficient conditions**. The question is whether self-harm *alone* is sufficient reason for the law to intervene. Mill states that there have to be other necessary conditions. The primary necessary condition is the lack of rational decision (i.e. a child or someone who is mentally ill).

So, if I engage willingly in a strange form of sexual activity however harmful this might appear to be, this is not a sufficient reason why I should not be free to make my own rational choices. I could argue that any form of self-harm is necessarily irrational, in which case if homosexuality could be shown to be psychologically or physically dangerous there would then be sufficient reason to intervene even if it did no harm to others.

ii Public harm
There are two related considerations:

- Mill argued that causing moral offence to others is not a sufficient reason for the law to outlaw it. However this begs the question. If many people are offended then might not this be a necessary condition of harm? If it could be shown that homosexuality causes widespread offence then there is good reason for the law to make it illegal.
- Can one really claim that private consenting acts have no effects on public morality? Some argue that all our actions and attitudes affect society. So, for instance, if I enjoy watching hard-core pornographic videos at home it will, inevitably, alter the way I think and treat others in public. This view challenges Mill's notion of a separate private morality.

There has been a long-standing view that same-sex relationships cause harm to public decency. In ancient Greece same-sex relationships between older men were considered to be corrupt, St Paul cites homosexuality as a reason why Roman society had degenerated morally (see p x below for a fuller analysis) and in the 18th century the 'Societies for the Reformation of Manners' were instrumental in the raids and closure of many 'molly houses' or gay clubs because they considered such places to corrupt public decency.

The argument that certain kinds of private acts do cause moral harm to society was argued by **Lord Devlin** in the well-known argument between himself and the legal philosopher **H L A Hart** over the issue of homosexuality in 1968. Devlin argued the following:

- All private morality has an effect on public morality. Public morality is necessary to keep society together and happy.
- Toleration of certain private acts does not necessarily have beneficial effects on society. For example just as treason is regarded as an attack on society so by analogy is deliberate lack of morality.
- Lack of morality can be judged by whatever the general public considers in strong terms to be offensive.

● Whatever the public finds strongly offensive is sufficient reason to outlaw certain private behaviour to protect public decency. Homosexuality is such an example.

Devlin's argument was criticised by Hart and others for the following reasons:

● It is not obvious that private acts do have a direct effect on public morality.
● Does the analogy of treason work? Hart argues that treason intentionally desires to undermine society, which is probably not the case for homosexual activity. The onus would have to be on Devlin and others to show that homosexuality does create a climate whereby people abandon their ordinary moral beliefs – such as their beliefs in marriage and family life.
● It is far from obvious when public sentiment reaches a consensus and whether a reasonable man would necessarily know or represent what others in society feel.
● Even if public consensus could be achieved, would it necessarily have a rational basis? For example, sodomy was feared in the 16th century because it was thought it would bring God's wrath on the nation in accordance with the Old Testament punishment of Sodom and Gomorrah. Is a religious reason sufficiently rational or really a form of irrational homophobia? Like racism, it might not be regarded as a sufficient reason for exclusion, even if it is a widely held opinion and strongly felt.

d) Physical harm

The discussion above has so far considered the cultural and moral challenges to a heterosexual society. But there are many who argue that leaving out any specifically moral evaluations, homosexuality (and male homosexuality in particular) is dangerous on empirical grounds as its sexual practices and lifestyle pose very great health risks to its participants and to society. Thomas Schmidt is representative of many conservative thinkers who take this line. His book *Straight and Narrow?* (1995) provides a full review of the present medical evidence. Most of his data is based on USA research and his survey leads to this general conclusion:

> But no honest look at current scientific research allows us to view homosexual practice as peaceable and harmless. For the vast majority of homosexual men, and for a significant number of homosexual women – even apart from the deadly plague of AIDS – sexual behavior is obsessive, psychopathological and destructive to the body. If there were no specific biblical principles to guide sexual behavior, these considerations alone would constitute a compelling argument against homosexual practice.

> T Schmidt *Straight and Narrow?* (1995) p130

Schmidt is effectively appealing to Mill's harm principle in terms of the physical risks that homosexual practices pose to both gays and heterosexuals. The argument has added weight that health risks are not just a private affair, but public and can and should be regulated by law.

i How many men are gay?

The question of number is significant because it suggest a possible scale of harm. In 1948 **Alfred Kinsey** (1894–1956) published the first comprehensive report on American sexual behaviour: *Sexual Behavior in the Human Male*. Amongst its many revelations which shocked and surprised American society was his conclusion that some 10% of those interviewed had been predominately homosexual for a period of up to three years before the survey. But he went on to show that only about 4% of those interviewed maintained a homosexual lifestyle consistently throughout adult life (and 2% for women).

More recent statistics are those of the National Opinion Research Center whose surveys between 1970–1990 came to the aggregate conclusions that 1.8% had experienced male to male sex during the previous year, 3.3% had had male to male sex occasionally or fairly often as male adults and 5–7% reported never having had male sex. But in active terms the percentage of USA population who are presently engaged in same-sex relationships is between 0.6–0.7% of the adult population. Put in other terms, out of a population of 180 million people some 1.5 million Americans have exclusive same-sex relations, in addition some three million have practised same-sex in the previous year.

ii Fidelity and permanency

Schmidt also found that based on the research of Bell and Weinberg (*Homosexualities* 1978) only about 10% of male and 28% of female same-sex relationships involved long-term cohabitation relationships. The conclusion is that the homosexual lifestyle is, as we noted briefly above, not of monogamy but either rapid serial 'monogamy' or multi-partnership. Schmidt's survey of various sources can be seen set out in Table 4.1:

Table 4.1: Gay and lesbian sexual relationships			
	Number of partners during a life time	Previous year	Length of relationship
male–male	74% 100 partners	55% 20 partners	7% more than 10 years
	41% 500 partners	30% 50 partners	38% never longer than 1 year
	28% 1000 partners		55% never longer than 2 years
woman–woman	60% 10 partners	3% 20 partners	20% more than 3 years
	2% 100 partners	1% 50 partners	

based on T Schmidt *Straight and Narrow?* pp105–108

Raw statistics mean very little in themselves. What they do appear to indicate is that lesbian lifestyle is based on longer term relationships than gay men. The report was written before the spread of AIDS which has modified gay sexual behaviour, but nevertheless gay culture, for some men, thrives far more on eroticism than lesbian lifestyle. More frequent changes of partner increase the likelihood of sexually transmitted diseases.

iii Sexual practices

The most common forms of sexual practices amongst male homosexuals according to the 1978 report of Bell and Weinberg are oral-genital contact (95%), mutual masturbation (80%), insertive anal intercourse (80%) and receptive anal intercourse (70%). Amongst women the most favoured techniques are mutual masturbation (80%) and oral genital-contact (80%). The popular view that lesbians rely on artificial penises or dildos for vaginal stimulation is in reality rare (3%). There are many health reasons why some, if not all of these practices are considered to be dangerous. Martin Levine describes what he calls 'gay clone' behaviour (Levine in Nye *Sexuality* p379) which in addition to exaggerated masculine looks (work boots, short hair cut, beard) also involves 'cruising' or 'tricking' (casual sex) by meeting at well-known gay bars and sex clubs. Tricking consists of violent anal and oral sex. But is it homosexuality as such which is being judged? From a utilitarian point of view, if tricking is considered risky for gays it must equally be so for heterosexuals.

iv Disease and health risks

A combination of factors have placed homosexuals in a much higher risk category than heterosexuals. As Table 4.1 indicates, a gay man is more likely to have multiple partners than his heterosexual counterpart, and more likely to be participating in sexual activity where disease is easily contracted and easily spread. The most devastating of these since the 1980s has been HIV/AIDS, but there are many other sexually transmitted diseases. The purpose here is not to analyse them all but to test the proposition whether homosexuality is harmful either to homosexuals themselves or to society as a whole.

The anus, for example, is far more prone to rupture and damage than the vagina. In addition it is far less sensitive than the vagina and so a man may not be aware of the damage that is being caused until infection has set in. The results can be incontinence, diarrhoea, haemorrhoids, ulcers and fissures that can lead to secondary infection.

It should be made clear that AIDS is no more a 'gay plague' than it is a heterosexual disease. However, where sexual practice is more high risk (e.g. amongst prostitutes, unprotected sex, drug users) then the likelihood of contracting HIV is greatly increased. AIDS has been common amongst homosexuals because as Table 4.1 indicates the greater number of partners increases the chances of contracting HIV. Furthermore, and as we have seen, the particular kind of sexual activities (oral-genital and anal intercourse) favoured in particular by gay men greatly increase the chances of the virus passing from body to body through fissures and abrasions in the anus, penis and mouth. The use of condoms for anal sex has helped, but a Dutch study (*American Journal of Public Health*, April 1992 cited by Schmidt p125) still calculates that there is a 6.1% chance of infection.

v Conclusions

The arrival of AIDS in America, where gays and lesbians live more openly in communities, has dramatically affected certain forms of homosexual lifestyle or 'experiments in living'. The physical threat of sexually transmitted disease through homosexuality to the wider community though is via those who are bisexual or who have experimented in same-sex relationships before choosing to be heterosexual. In numerical terms homosexuality poses only a very small direct threat to society as a whole. Critics argue that indirectly homosexuality encourages promiscuous and dangerous sexual practices in the wider society. For instance, if the law of homosexual consent in Britain were to be lowered it would also permit legal anal sex for all adults from the age of 16. The challenge still remains for any liberal legislator to protect individuals from actual physical 'harm' and to distinguish general distaste from real moral offence.

3 Theological considerations

KEY ISSUE

● Why does Christian theology have such sharply differing views about homosexuality?

Homosexuality presents all the churches with a considerable moral and spiritual challenge. For traditionalists the Bible and Christian tradition have consistently condemned homosexual behaviour. But liberal Christians (that is those who incorporate current insights of philosophy, science and psychology) argue that what is meant by 'homosexuality' today is very different from the situation in the past and so the Church must revise its views in the light of present experience.

a) Church attitudes

Homosexuality, more than any other area of sexual ethics at present, challenges theology to consider just what it means to be a sexual person living a full life in God's image. There is no consensus. There are those who argue that the nature of the homosexual lifestyle means that it will always fall short of what God requires, whereas others see in same-sex love a special kind of friendship which may even have something to teach heterosexual relationships. Recent Church reports on sexuality reflect the current tension between traditional and liberal attitudes to homosexuality.

i Church of England
Take for instance the conclusions from the statement made by the Church of England's House of Bishops, *Issues in Human Sexuality* (1991):

1   There is, therefore, in Scripture an evolving convergence on the ideal life-long, monogamous, heterosexual union as the setting intended by God for the proper development of men and women as sexual beings. Sexual activity of any kind outside marriage comes to be seen as sinful,
5   and homosexual practice as especially dishonourable (p18)... The first [principle] is that homophile orientation and its expression in sexual activity does not constitute a parallel and alternative form of human sexuality as complete within the terms of the created order as the heterosexual (p40)... This leads directly to our second fundamental
10   principle, laid upon us by the truths at the very heart of the faith; homosexual people are in every way as valuable to and as valued by God as heterosexual people. God loves us all alike, and has for each of us a range of possibilities within his design for the universe (p41)... Of

Christian homophiles some are clear that the way they must follow to
15   fulfil this calling is to witness to God's general will for human sexuality
by a life of abstinence. In the power of the Holy Spirit and out of love
for Christ they embrace the self-denial involved, gladly and trustfully
opening themselves to the power of God's grace to order and fulfil
their personalities within this way of life (p41)... At the same time
20   there are others who are conscientiously convinced that this way of
abstinence is not best for them, and that they have more hope of
growing in love for God and neighbour with the help of a loving and
faithful homophile partnership, in intention lifelong, where mutual self-
giving includes the physical expression of their attachment (p41)... We
25   have, therefore, to say that in our considered judgement the clergy
cannot claim the liberty to enter into sexually active homophile
relationships. Because of the distinctive nature of their calling, status
and consecration, to allow such a claim on their part would be seen as
placing that way of life in all respects on a par with heterosexual
30   marriage as a reflection of God's purposes in creation. The Church
cannot accept such parity and remain faithful to the insights which God
has given it through Scripture, tradition and reasoned reflection on
experience (p45)...

The Church of England, therefore, acknowledges that there are those
who are homosexual not by choice but by orientation and that they
must be given full pastoral acceptance into church communities. But
the least satisfactory argument rests on homosexual physical sexual
relationships. Whereas it is felt that this may be necessary for a full
relationship for the laity (non-ordained) it is not permissible for
priests and bishops because at the heart of the Christian vocation
homosexuality falls short of the ideal. The report uneasily reflects the
tension between those who look to the Bible as the sole source of
God's revelation and traditionally oppose homosexual practice and
those who feel that human conscience should be guided by our
present knowledge of biology and psychology. Unfortunately, despite
the genuine desire to move the debate on, this report is no clearer
than several other earlier reports.

ii Roman Catholic

The Roman Catholic Church is more explicit in its conclusions.
Homosexuality is contrary to Scripture and natural law, but the
Catechism (1994) today accepts the notion that some people are, for
reasons which are unclear, born with homosexual inclinations. But
unlike the Church of England, their vocation must be to a life of
sexual **chastity**:

1   The number of men and women who have deep-seated homosexual
tendencies is not negligible. They do not choose their homosexual
condition; for most of them it is a trial. They must be accepted with
respect, compassion and sensitivity... Homosexual persons are called

5 to chastity. By virtues of self-mastery that teach them inner freedom, at
   times by the support of disinterested friendship, by prayer and
   sacramental grace, they can and should gradually and resolutely
   approach Christian perfection.

The Catechism of the Catholic Church (1994) p505

The *Catechism* marks a change in emphasis from earlier Catholic
teaching in 1975:

1 At the present time there are those who, basing themselves on
   observations in the psychological order, have begun to judge indulgently,
   and even to excuse completely, homosexual relations between certain
   people. This they do in opposition of the Magesterium and to the moral
5 sense of the Christian people.

Declaration on Certain Questions concerning Sexual Ethics p11

The *magesterium* (the official teaching of the Catholic Church) in both
documents maintains that homosexuality is technically 'intrinsically
disordered' – that is from the point of view of natural law
homosexuality is objectively morally wrong and if practised would
lead to grave sin. But the *Catechism* holds a more sympathetic pastoral
view that, despite this condition, the homosexual can live a sexually
chaste life to achieve God's salvation. The Church's more developed
theology of the single life (in the priesthood for instance) enables it
to distinguish a fulfilled (though homosexual) life from a physical
sexual relationship. The latter is confined through marriage
exclusively to heterosexual couples (see Chapter 4).

b) Interpreting the Biblical texts

One of the major tensions in the debate is the exact interpretation of
the few but significant Biblical texts which are considered to deal
explicitly with homosexuality. In this section we shall look only at
these passages, but a Biblical theology which develops a sexual ethic
must go wider than this and consider human relationships within a
broader theology. For the sake of argument, we shall consider two
views: the conservative/traditionalist represented by Thomas Schmidt
in *Straight and Narrow?* (1995) and the liberal/revisionist represented
by William Countryman in *Dirt, Greed and Sex* (1988).

i Sodom and Gomorrah/Gibeah

There are two remarkably similar stories in the Old Testament
(Genesis 19:1–8; Judges 19:16–30) both of which recount an incident
where it appears that the men of a town wish to rape the male
visitor(s). In both stories the host offers them his virgin daughter(s)
to be gang raped instead. Subsequently Sodom and Gomorrah were
both destroyed for their sins (of which this was one example) and so

this story in particular has become synonymous in Christian tradition for the evil of homosexual sex. The much-disputed verses are:

> 'Where are the men who came to you tonight? Bring them out to us, that we might know them.' (Genesis 19:5)

> 'Bring out the man who came into your house, that we may know him.' (Judges 19:22)

● **A question of hospitality**. The revisionist interpretation argues that the setting for both stories focuses on the lack of hospitality. We should remember that in those days hospitality for the traveller was considered to be a very great duty. Both narrators are at pains to highlight the gross abrogation of this duty. 'He went in and sat down in the open square of the city; for no man took them into his house to spend the night' (Judges 19:15). With this is in mind when the men of the city demand to 'know' the visitor(s) how should this be interpreted? The Hebrew 'yada', to 'know', can be used in its sexual sense, but in many cases it can mean to enquire (i.e. to find out more of the credentials of the travellers especially as their hosts are themselves both aliens to the city) and as Countryman points out when the Levite recounts the story he interprets 'know' to mean 'kill': 'they meant to kill me, and ravished my concubine and she is dead' (Judges 20:5).

The stories are therefore illustrations of wickedness of the townspeople and not directly about homosexuality. For instance, Ezekiel 16:49–50 cites Sodom as a place whose abominations included failure to help the poor and needy, and in the New Testament Jesus chooses Sodom's notorious lack of hospitality as an example of the events which will be particularly judged on the Day of Judgement:

> And if anyone will not receive you or listen to your words, shake off the dust from under your feet as you leave that house or town. Truly, I say to you, it shall be more tolerable on the day of judgement for the land of Sodom and Gomorrah than for that town.
>
> Matthew 10:14–15

● **Gang rape**. Even if the sin of Sodom and Gibeah is due to the lack of hospitality, nevertheless both stories rely on sexual abuse to convey the depth of depravity to which both sets of citizens have sunk. In the case of the Levite his concubine is so badly raped that she dies, and Lot offers his virgin daughters for them to rape. At the very least, then, the stories condemn homosexual rape but primarily because of its violence. As Countryman argues, the stories tell us little about homosexuality because the authors' interests are not concerned with moral sexual purity, but violence against strangers. Even if these stories were to condemn homosexual behaviour, it would not judge all homosexual relationships (as we would understand them today) but the violence of rape. Countryman concludes:

1 Condemnation of violence, even where it appears likely that it would
have included homosexual rape, can hardly be equated with a universal
condemnation of homosexuality or even homosexual acts… If one asks
whether the punishment visited on Sodom or on Gibeah was
5 occasioned by impurity or by violence against strangers, it is clear in
both cases that only the latter is possible.

L W Countryman *Dirt, Greed and Sex* (1996) p31

● **Sexual sin**. Despite the arguments above, many commentators ancient
and modern do regard Sodom as a condemnation of homophile sexual
sin. The repetition of the story in Judges with its heightened account of
the concubine's rape already suggests the sexual element of the story.
By the first century CE the *Testament of the Twelve Patriarchs* illustrates
the 'fornication of Sodom' with evil and God's judgement (see *Testament
of Benjamin* 9:1) and the Jewish commentator and scholar Philo clearly
cites Sodom as an explicit example of same-sex vice. Schmidt concedes
with Countryman that the story of Sodom does not describe
homosexual relationships as such, but warns that we should note that it
is a corrupt and sinful society in which same-sex sexual perversion of
this kind takes place that gives the story its continuing teaching power
today.

ii Leviticus and the Holiness Code

The passages which deal far more explicitly with homosexuality form
part of what is generally referred to by scholars as the 'Holiness Code'
(Leviticus 17–26). The purpose of the code is to distinguish the
Israelites from the foreign practices of the Canaanites (Leviticus
18:1–3) who also occupy the land which they inhabit. The intention
of the author is to differentiate all the false religious practices of the
cult of the Canaanites from the true worship of the Israelites.

And you shall not lie with a male as with a woman; it is an abomination

Leviticus 18:22

If a man lies with a male as with a woman, both of them have committed
an abomination; they shall be put to death, their blood is upon them.

Leviticus 20:13

● **Cult prostitution**. Leviticus 18 lists the offences which will
contaminate the land. In Chapter 20 the list is repeated but this time
with the inclusion of the extreme punishments for those who offend
(including children who curse their parents, adulterers, incest, bestiality
and homosexuality) as a symbol of those who are cut off from the
community of Israel. Leviticus condemns all acts which 'confuse' the
natural order: a field must contain one kind of seed, a garment one set
of fibres and so on. Homosexuality is therefore condemned on two

scores. Firstly, that it confuses sexual roles, because one of the men has to play the role of the woman. Secondly, the Hebrew term used in a similar context (e.g. Deuteronomy 23:17) 'qadesh' almost certainly refers to the Canaanite practice of having sex with male prostitutes in the temple. So, the code condemns homosexual sex because of its idolatrous association with Canaanite cult practice; this is not the same as condemning all homosexual relationships.

● **Moral law**. But for many Countryman's argument is too weak. What Leviticus describes is not simply a custom to be avoided to aid identification, but something which is morally reprehensible. Schmidt doubts whether by the time of the 1st century Christians would have made the kind of subtle distinctions the modern revisionist has in mind. In any case, Leviticus 18 and 20 should be read including Leviticus 19, a chapter entirely devoted to moral laws concerning injustice to the poor, stealing and revenge. Seen in this context all forms of homosexuality must be considered morally wrong.

iii The arsenkoitai and malakoi

Jesus only explicitly criticises one kind of sexual sin and that is adultery (Matthew 5:27–30; John 8:1–11) – the argument from silence means that either he accepts the current view that homosexuality was wrong, or that it simply was not a concern amongst Jews. By contrast, once Paul and others took Christianity outside the confines of Israel into the Greek-Roman world one of the problems they faced was whether same-sex relations were commensurate with Christian holiness. In a list of vices which echoes the Ten Commandments, Paul writes to the Greek converts at Corinth:

1   Do you not know that the unrighteous will not inherit the kingdom of God? Do not be deceived; neither the immoral, nor idolaters, nor adulterers, nor sexual perverts [malakoi / arsenkoitai], nor thieves, nor the greedy, nor drunkards, nor revilers, nor robbers will inherit the
5   kingdom of God. And such were some of you. But you were washed, you were sanctified, you were justified in the name of the Lord Jesus Christ in the Spirit of our God.

1 Corinthians 6:9–11

The various translations of the text illustrate the problem of two Greek words: 'malakoi' (soft) and 'arsenkoitai' (males who have sexual intercourse). The Revised Standard Version of the Bible first translated these two words as 'homosexual' and then in a revised edition as 'sexual perverts'. The only other place in the New Testament where 'arsenkoitai' is used (1 Timothy 1:10) in a similar list the author does not use malakoi in conjunction with it.

● Some contend that 'malakoi' and 'arsenkoitai' represent the passive (soft) and active partners in the homosexual relationship – in a way reminiscent of the Levitical dislike of mixing opposites (see above).

However, as I Timothy does not use 'malakoi' this is unlikely. Countryman argues that as the Greeks permitted same-sex relationships equally as heterosexual relationships, it is unlikely they would have had a word which would have described an exclusively homosexual act.

● Others argue that 'malakoi' refers to masturbation and 'arsenkoitai' to male prostitution. Countryman comments that even though it is 'unclear whether Paul's use of the term was meant to condemn them for homosexual acts of prostitution or for both' (p119) given the lack of usage of the words in the Greek world this translation is preferable to the explicit homosexual interpretation outlined above.

● Schmidt argues that it is no coincidence that Paul includes these terms in his list just after mentioning adultery. Adultery is universally condemned because it undermines marriage and the family. Homosexual behaviour – whether with prostitutes or not – is equivalent to the sin of adultery. An intriguing idea is that 'arsenkoitai' is a newly invented term based on the Greek translation (the Septuagint) of the Old Testament from Leviticus 18:22 and 20:13 where the two terms 'arsenos' and 'koiten' are used to translate the Hebrew words. It is possible that Paul himself compounded the two words to form a new technical term to refer to same-sex behaviour. Because Schmidt considers Leviticus' prohibition of homosexual behaviour is for moral reasons and not just for purity (see above), it follows that he also considers Paul's language here to be a decisive condemnation of homosexuality.

iv Gentiles and sin

One passage, though, does seem to refer explicitly to homosexual behaviour. Paul writes his letter to the Christian community at Rome although he has not yet visited them in person. Rome represents the goal of his mission to the Gentiles and the focus of his message. His letter picks its way through the complexities of theology for a diverse audience comprising Jewish-Christian converts and Greek/Roman-Christians. In the first two chapters Paul sets himself the task to show how all have had access to God's revelation, but all – Jew and Gentile – have fallen short. The first chapter is aimed at the non-Jew and it is in this context that Paul writes:

1   For the wrath of God is revealed from heaven against all ungodliness and wickedness of men who by their wickedness suppress the truth (1:18) ... Claiming to be wise, they became fools, and exchanged the glory of the immortal God for images resembling mortal man or birds
5   or animals or reptiles. Therefore God gave them up in the lusts [epithymia] of their hearts to impurity, to dishonouring of their bodies among themselves (1:22–25) ... For this reason God gave them up to dishonourable passions. Their women exchanged natural relations for unnatural, and the men likewise gave up natural relations with women
10   and were consumed with passion for one another, men committing

shameless acts with men and receiving in their own persons the due
penalty for their error (1:26–27)

Romans 1:18–27

● **Purity codes and sin**. Countryman argues that Paul's argument here
is essentially a rhetorical device. The problem for the early Jewish-
Christians was accepting Gentile converts who did not observe the
purity codes of the Jews (food, table-fellowship, circumcision and so on).
By focusing on the notorious sexual impropriety or 'dirtiness' of the
Roman-Greek culture Paul is able to win over his Jewish-Christian
audience (Romans 1) and then with a clever twist of the argument
accuse them of being equally sinful and equally open to God's
judgement:

O man, whoever you are, when you judge another; for in passing
judgment upon him you condemn yourself, because you, the judge, are
doing the very same things.

Romans 2:1

So, Paul hopes to win the sympathies of his Jewish-Christian audience
by placing the Gentile sexual culture in the context of their own
Jewish weaknesses. He hopes they will realise that all Christians see
themselves falling short of the mark. So, homosexual behaviour is not
condemned because it is intrinsically sinful, but because it offends
against the Levitical purity laws. As Paul finally comments in Romans
14:14 ('I know and am persuaded in the Lord Jesus that nothing is
unclean in itself; but it is unclean for any one who thinks it unclean')
these laws cannot in themselves be a bar to salvation. Therefore,
Countryman concludes, modern revulsion to homosexuality is not a
moral judgement, but a social experience which, in time, can change.
If there are moral judgements to be made about homosexuality they
should surely be based on the quality of the relationship and not on
our like or dislike of physical sexual practices.

1 To deny an entire class of human beings the right peaceably and without
harming others to pursue the kind of sexuality that corresponds to
their nature is a perversion of the gospel. Like the insistence of some
on the circumcising of Gentile converts, it makes the keeping of purity
5 rules a condition of grace.

L W Countryman *Dirt, Greed and Sex* (1996) p244

● **Sin is sin**. But for many conservative theologians the liberal-revisionist
interpretation simply does not give sufficient weight to the gravity of sin
(and correspondingly to redemption). The situation which Paul sketches
is not about cultural differences based on likes and dislikes but about
behaviour which is contrary to the divine created order which directly
affects society itself. The use of the Greek term '*epithymia*' refers to the
kind of vices which are at the heart of social corruption and

disintegration. Homosexuality is directly contrary to the establishment of marriage and the family as the corner-stone of society. This is reinforced by an unusual detail in these verses. Paul first introduces his judgement on homosexuality by referring to lesbian sex which was heavily frowned upon by Roman society and so it follows that Paul is making a very particular case in which male same-sex relationships are being presented to be equally reprehensible even by Gentile standards.

- **Contrary to creation and marriage**. Three times Paul uses the phrase 'God gave them up' each time to Gentile activity which is contrary to the 'invisible order' of the creation. The verse which causes more controversy than any other is *'para physin'* often translated as 'unnatural'. Schmidt argues that it is too weak a translation to render *'physin'* as 'custom' and cites a number of classical writers who use the phrase *'para physin'* specifically to contrast homosexual behaviour with heterosexual sex according to nature itself. Furthermore Paul echoes the sentiments of the first century Jewish writer of the *Wisdom of Solomon* (chapters 13–14) that sexual perversion is directly contrary to creation; it is not a strange custom but rebellion against God. Finally Paul talks of the Gentiles being 'consumed with passion for one another', a phrase which would normally be appropriate in heterosexual marriage but applied here to gay and lesbian relationships. Schmidt argues that Paul has avoided language which might refer to the Roman practice of male prostitution and pederasty and instead deliberately 'exchanged' marital relations for the corruption homosexuality. In other words what Paul condemns are men and women living a homosexual lifestyle which deliberately undermines the natural order represented by heterosexual family life.

c) Being Christian and homosexual

KEY ISSUE

- Is homosexuality unnatural and contrary to the Christian idea of love and marriage?

Discussion of Biblical texts illustrates the difficulty which many Christians find responding to homosexuality. Even those who consider themselves to live by a 'Bible morality' find that the texts are sometimes ambiguous. There are considerable differences of opinion as to what extent Jesus' teaching adapted or even dispensed with the commands of the Old Testament. So the questions posed here consider whether being a practising homosexual and Christian is possible within the wider range of Christian thought.

i Natural law

We have seen that attitudes to same-sex lifestyle have been determined by more than the simple act of anal or oral sex. However in the first instance, the natural law tradition stemming from **Thomas Aquinas** (*c*1225–1274), does explicitly condemn anal and oral sex because it thwarts the *telos* or purpose of sexual intercourse to have children.

1   It is evident from this that every emission of semen, in such a way that generation cannot follow, is contrary to the good of man. And if this be done deliberately, it must be a sin. Now, I am speaking of a way from which, in itself, generation could not result; such would be any emission
5   of semen apart from the natural union of male and female...Moreover, these views which have just been given have a solid basis in divine authority. That the emission of semen under conditions in which offspring cannot follow is illicit is quite clear. There is the text of Leviticus (18:22–23) 'thou shalt not lie with mankind as with
10   womankind...'

T Aquinas *Summa Contra Gentiles* 3.2. 122
quoted in R Gill *A Textbook of Christian Ethics* (1995) pp 484–86

But a natural law defence is considered badly flawed and ultimately unsatisfactory. For instance:

- The notion of a *telos* is ambiguous. Sex may equally be regarded purposeful for unitive or loving ends. If the lack of intent to reproduce does not condemn a heterosexual relationship, it could equally be applied to a homosexual one.
- Aquinas' argument is a judgement on all sexual acts which are conducted without the intention to reproduce. This is not a judgement on homosexual orientation as such but all (heterosexual as well) anal/oral sex or sex using contraception.
- Modern scientific consensus does not regard homosexuality to be a deviant pathology. Being in a minority is not in itself contrary to any natural law any more than being left-handed.
- Natural law is always subject to the criticism of the 'naturalistic fallacy'. It is incoherent to derive from statements of fact (first order) statements of value (second order). So, for instance it is fallacious to move from the biological fact that humans have reproductive organs and jump to an abstract law that we must reproduce. Our attitudes to sex are based on social expectation not intrinsic laws. However, for certain Christians, Christian principles based on the Bible and tradition may still condemn homosexuality, but it cannot be on the grounds that homosexuality is unnatural.

ii Marriage and family

As we have seen (above page 69) a considerable objection to homosexual behaviour is that gays and lesbians in sexual relationships are unable to fulfil the Christian aims of marriage, namely to rear children, offer mutual support, and have a faithful monogamous sexual relationship (see also Table 4.1). Moreover, as marriage is the basis for the family as a 'domestic church', a homosexual relationship ultimately lacks the creative and spiritual dimension which is to be found in a Christian heterosexual family. For the family to function as a 'domestic church' children need the complementary upbringing of male and female, which mirrors the Christ–Church, husband–wife, parents–child relationship (Ephesians 5:21–6:2). Children, as David Brown argues, are necessary to direct a couple's love outwards so that 'through the family the possibility of Christian love is conveyed from generation to generation' (*Choices* p108). Brown acknowledges that this doesn't prohibit childless couples any more than homosexual couples from adopting a child but:

> There is still this difference from the heterosexual couple, that there is no natural tendency for them to seek such an outlet, since a desire for children or a substitute for them is no part of the motivation upon which their relationship is based.
>
> D Brown *Choices: Ethics and the Chrisitian* (1983) p109

The alternative is celibate love, where the homosexual's creative energy can be directed into the 'caring professions, teaching, medicine and the Church' (*Choices: Ethics and the Christian* p109) indeed any job which reduces introversion and isolation.

- The notion of family is considerably more than legal and kinship ties. A household comprises those who have common duties and responsibilities to each other. If Christian heterosexual couples can adopt or even have children through donors and be considered a family, then it follows that a homosexual couple are equally capable of doing the same.
- How is friendship to be defined? If there is no same-sex contact then all forms of hugging, kissing or simply sharing a house with some one whom one deeply cares for would surely be wrong. Sexuality covers a wide range of human experience. The Old Testament describes the relationship of David and Jonathan 'where the soul of Jonathan was knit to the soul of David, and Jonathan loved him as his own soul' (1 Samuel 18:1) The relationship, though not necessarily gay, is clearly sexual.
- The call to celibacy is not a vocation all share. Where two homosexual committed people love each other in faithfulness then its expression physically and spiritually cannot and should not be considered to 'fall short' or to be the 'lesser good'. To deny the physical aspect of a relationship through 'sublimation' returns the church to its ancient view based on Augustine's dualistic notion that the body is sinful whereas the soul is pure. To be a whole person means being able to express oneself (heterosexually and homosexually), physically and spiritually.

iii Creation and redemption

In his critique of the five Church reports on sexuality, Michael Banner criticised them all for failing to return to and clarify the Biblical Christian doctrine of creation (*Christian Ethics and Contemporary Moral Problems* 1999 pp 260–261). Banner recommends consideration of the great reform theologian **Karl Barth (1886–1968)** who sees in nature the complementary relationship of God and world, the God–man covenant expressed in the created union of man and woman. If it is only the male–female paradigm through which God effects salvation should the churches give a categorical 'no' to homosexuality? A response might lie in Banner's reminder that a doctrine of creation is also a doctrine of redemption of a fallen world. For in St Paul's central teaching on God's grace, all human sins are removed regardless of class, race and gender. The list does not specifically exclude any sexual category.

> For as many of you as were baptised into Christ have put on Christ. There is neither Jew nor Greek, there is neither slave nor free, there is neither male nor female; for you are all one in Christ Jesus.
>
> Galatians 3:27–28

iv Justice and liberation

Another way of considering the inclusion of homosexuals within Christian salvation is by looking at the story of redemption from Genesis (the fall of humans) to the liberation of the Jews in the book of Exodus. In particular, the significance of the story for the **liberation theologian** is that it tells of an actual enslaved people (Israel) freed from bondage in Egypt and taken to the promised land. Salvation is not an abstract idea for the story speaks in actual historical terms. Gay Christian liberation identifies with this kind of theology – a theology of doing (*praxis*).

- For the Old Testament prophets redemption meant real justice. For the modern Christian gays and lesbians the Christian gospel must be extended to be inclusive of another group in society who for too long have experienced alienation and injustice.
- Jesus' own life illustrated his concern with the marginalised and those excluded because of their sex and sexual activities. He ate with the disenfranchised and interceded on behalf of the woman about to be stoned to death because of her adultery (John 8:1–11).

Answering structured and essay questions

Questions

1. **a)** Why is homosexuality a political as well as a moral issue?
   b) Assess the idea that we should be free to behave in whatever sexual way we wish.
2. **a)** Explain why theologians are divided over whether the Bible condemns homosexuality or not.
   b) 'If a gay or lesbian relationship is loving and committed then it cannot be wrong.' Discuss.
3. Discuss whether the debate about homosexuality is purely a question of human rights.
4. 'Homosexuality is unnatural and opposed to the Christian idea of love and marriage.' Discuss.
5. 'If boxing is dangerous then it should be made illegal. If homosexuality is dangerous it also should be made illegal.' Discuss.

Essay skills

Broadly there are two arguments here. The first is that based on natural law or Christian ethics, that homosexuality is intrinsically wrong. The second is that morality is essentially a private affair and homosexuality should be tolerated. Essays need to state clearly how a particular view is derived and why in many cases it often begs the question (use this phrase) e.g. why is the liberal principle necessarily right? Why is toleration good? Who judges when harm is really harmful? You should point out that empirical (factual) evidence does not mean much in itself (such as the number of people who are homosexual) unless used as part of a wider argument. Try also to distinguish between notions of gay, lesbian and queer to show that homosexuality means different things to different people. If you are concentrating more on the theological arguments then it is important to distinguish between conservative/traditional and liberal views.

Summary of secular liberal and theological responses to homosexuality

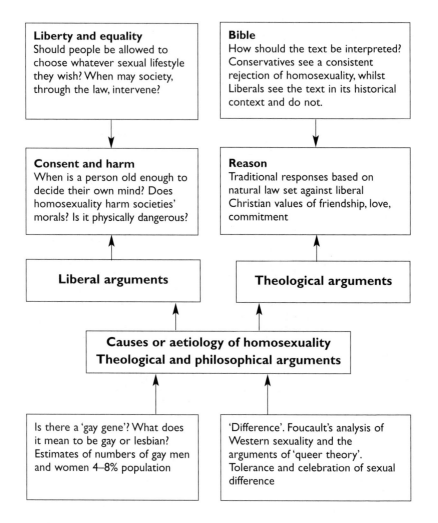

Liberty and equality
Should people be allowed to choose whatever sexual lifestyle they wish? When may society, through the law, intervene?

Bible
How should the text be interpreted? Conservatives see a consistent rejection of homosexuality, whilst Liberals see the text in its historical context and do not.

Consent and harm
When is a person old enough to decide their own mind? Does homosexuality harm societies' morals? Is it physically dangerous?

Reason
Traditional responses based on natural law set against liberal Christian values of friendship, love, commitment

Liberal arguments

Theological arguments

Causes or aetiology of homosexuality
Theological and philosophical arguments

Is there a 'gay gene'? What does it mean to be gay or lesbian? Estimates of numbers of gay men and women 4–8% population

'Difference'. Foucault's analysis of Western sexuality and the arguments of 'queer theory'. Tolerance and celebration of sexual difference

5 Marriage and divorce

KEYWORDS

annulment or nullity – in Roman Catholic theology a marriage may be deemed never to have been fully instituted if later it can be demonstrated that the intention to marry was lacking. 'Diriment' means to nullify

divorce – is a broad term which can refer to annulment, separation and divorce. Today it is generally taken to refer to the legal dissolving of the marriage bond and promises

fornication – refers to illicit sex which takes place between people who are not married. Pre-marital (i.e. sex before marriage) is regarded by many Christians to be fornication

indissoluble – a marriage which is dissoluble cannot be ended through divorce. The Christian tradition of marriage is essentially indissolubilist

irretrievable breakdown – the term used in many divorce laws as the single fault basis for divorce

Matthean exception – refers to a passage in Matthew's gospel (Matthew 19:19) where divorce is permitted on grounds of 'unchastity' – this is frequently taken to mean adultery, although the Greek word '*porneia*' is unclear

Pauline privilege – refers to St Paul's permission to divorce where either husband or wife are not Christian (1 Corinthians 7:15)

sacrament – a Christian religious ceremony in which symbolic actions and words confer God's grace or love. In Roman Catholicism marriage is a sacrament. It is not usually regarded as a sacrament in the Protestant Churches

separation – traditionally there are two kinds of separation: *a mensa et thoro* (Latin from board and lodge). In church and secular law this is judicial separation whereby husband and wife are released from their obligations to each other. *A vincula* (Latin from the bond) dissolves the marriage bond and is what is meant by divorce today

unitive – the purpose of marriage (and sex) is for companionship and love. In Christian thought this refers to heterosexual, monogamous and life-long union

1 Why marry?

KEY ISSUE

● Have attitudes to marriage in the past always been consistent?

In 1536, shortly after he had permitted divorce in his church, Martin Luther found that a major occupation was finding the emotional energy to sustain marriages. He is reported to have said when adjudicating a divorce petition:

> Good God, what a bother these matrimonial cases are to us! It takes great effort and labour to get couples together. Afterwards it requires even more pains to keep them together.
>
> quoted in *Untying the Knot*, R Phillips (1991) p15

In the past, as today, the most important institution through which men and women could express themselves sexually was in marriage. Whatever ceremonies accompany marriage, the most significant aspect is the shift in the status of the couple; for this to become significant it requires the acknowledgement of the community. But marriage is not just one particular public moment, for the couple it is one in a series of moments that continue into the new life spent together as companions, lovers, parents and friends.

a) Reasons for marriage

But what are the moral or social reasons for marriage today? In the contemporary world many of the reasons which made marriage a necessity in the past have largely been replaced – sex is no longer confined to one partner; ownership of property is available to men and women; women in the West can have security and income on an equal footing with men. Marriage may be a useful tool of the state to regularise relationships, to protect children and administer rights of property, but since many people today consider living together or **cohabitation** as a natural way to express themselves sexually, the moral reasons for marriage may appear obscure and old-fashioned.

Is marriage better than cohabitation or morally the right way in which adult relationships should take place? Which of the following would you consider to be the essential reasons for marriage:

● sharing interests, hobbies and for companionship
● a stable relationship for bringing up children
● long term commitment based on love and trust
● the best kind of relationship for sex
● having the security and backing of the law
● having more money to set up home.

b) Shifting attitudes to marriage and divorce

The development of marriage and divorce in the West has a long and complicated history. No discussion of the present state of marriage and divorce can be given without first considering it from the perspective of Christianity and more specifically from within the Catholic Church. From the adoption of Christianity by Constantine in 320 CE the Catholic tradition gradually came to set the moral and legal standards of the West. At the Reformation, the Catholic Church lost some of its control in Europe, but even then subsequent legislation was based on Catholic teaching.

Perhaps the single most important change has been to regard marriage as a special form of companionship based on a mutual relationship rather than a legal contract for the production of children.

i St Paul (c 50 CE)

The Western Christian tradition is based on the writings of Paul from the New Testament. Paul had only grudgingly accepted marriage as the means by which sexual desire could be legitimately expressed. Paul considers marriage at length in 1 Corinthians 7. It is clear early on in the chapter that he regards the single state to be superior to the married. He states that husband and wife have sexual duties to each other which should not be denied or else lust will lead to lack of control and detract each partner from their spiritual duties. Despite this positive view, Paul still feels that his own celibate (single, unmarried) life is better, 'I wish that all were as I myself am. But each has his own special gift from God, one of one kind and one of another.' (1 Corinthians 7:7). This leads to the conclusion that marriage is a more lowly state than being unmarried and chaste:

> To the unmarried and the widows I say that it is well for them to remain single as I do. But if they cannot exercise self-control, they should marry. For it is better to marry than to be aflame with passion.
>
> I Corinthians 7:8–9

Whatever Paul may have had in mind in his letter (see Marriage and the Bible below, page xx) Paul's influence through Augustine and the Western tradition established a view of marriage and sex which has only recently been reinterpreted. Because sex is associated with sin the primary purpose of marriage is a means of containing it. Many regard Paul and then Augustine to have done huge damage to Western attitudes to sex.

ii Catholic Church and natural law

Augustine (354–430 CE) was writing at a time when he was particularly involved with a debate with a group of heretical Christians called the Pelagians. The Pelagians rejected the idea of original sin whereas Augustine regarded sex as the manifestation of lust and self-centredness (or 'concupiscence') and proof of the punishment for sin being passed on from one generation to the next. As a dualist he believed that there is a distinction between the body (sinful) and the soul (good). But at the same time, Augustine took God's command in the Old Testament to 'be fruitful and multiply' (Genesis 1:28) as the divine and natural law that humans should procreate (to produce children). So, marriage is good because it is ordained by God. These two ideas provided the basis for Augustine's interpretation of St Paul to mean that the purpose or **goods** of marriage are:

● to **procreate** i.e. to have children
● to provide **fidelity** or faithfulness between husband and wife
● to be a **sacrament** as a means for God's grace to overcome sin and 'order' or control the sexual urge.

So, in summary Augustine's two works *de Bono Conjugali* (401) and *De Nuptiis et Concupiscentia* (421) present marriage as the means of containing sexual sin and human waywardness, and although marriage depends on commitment and faithfulness love is not a primary concern even though it may symbolise the perfect human relationship in Paradise before the Fall.

Aquinas (*c*1225–1274 CE) adopted and adapted Augustine. He was less influenced by the sharp body-spirit dualism of Augustine and put less emphasis on marriage as the containment of sin. He extended the natural law argument and maintained that as the primary reason for sex is for the procreation of children then the purpose of marriage is to provide the most stable environment for them to be brought up in. He argues that men naturally wish to remain with the woman after intercourse to help with the bringing up of the children. Children need to be instructed by the man:

I   Now a woman alone is not adequate to this task; rather, this demands the work of a husband, in whom reason is more developed for giving instruction and strength is more available for giving punishment... Hence, since among all animals it is necessary for the male and female to
5   remain together as long as the work of the father is needed by the offspring, it is natural to the human being for the man to establish a lasting association with a designated woman, over no short period of time. Now, we call this society matrimony. Therefore matrimony is natural for man, and promiscuous performance of the sexual act, outside
10 matrimony is contrary to man's good. For this reason it must be a sin.

Aquinas *Summa Contra Gentiles* 3.2
quoted in *A Textbook of Christian Ethics* by R Gill (1995) p486

Aquinas' dependency on natural law then leads him to argue why marriage should be life-long. He argues that the wife needs a husband to control her 'since the male is both more perfect in reasoning and stronger in his powers' (see Gill *Texts* p488, and Chapter 2 page xx). Until 1891 in Britain it was lawful for a husband to use moderate force to chastise his wife. But Aquinas also argues that the husband has a natural duty to look after his wife after she has passed childbearing age because without her primary function no man would want her. Natural justice demands that the woman should be cared for until death. Marriage is the basis for a life based on trust, mutual obligation and stability.

iii The Protestant tradition
The term 'Protestant' is taken here to represent the main traditions which came about as a protest against the Roman Catholic Church in the 16th century, after the term used at the Diet of Speyer in 1529. The main strands of Protestantism are Lutheranism and Calvinism. The Church of England and Anglicanism (i.e. the churches which have a common ancestry in the Church of England) came about partly because of Henry VIII's rejection of the papal authority to grant him annulment for his marriage. But severing of papal authority did not mean a rejection of its Catholic heritage. Later developments in the Church adopted Protestant ideas and it is common for many Anglicans to think of themselves as 'Protestants'. Many, though, stress the Church's Catholic origins. This is an important distinction, because until the 19th century, the Church of England's influence on the country's laws of marriage and divorce were largely at odds with Protestant Europe.

Despite the variety of views within the Protestant Churches, the churches were united in their common aims of seeing:

- The **Bible** as the primary source of Christian truth (and so a greatly reduced significance of natural law and church tradition).
- The minimising of church practices – especially to the over importance laid on the **sacraments** (most regarded only holy communion and baptism as the two Biblical sacraments).
- A **personal relationship** with God as the chief purpose of religion based on faith.

In most cases the reformers chose **adultery** (i.e. when a married person has a sexual relationship with some one who is not either their husband or wife) as the primary grounds for divorce. Some such as **Ulrich Zwingli** (1484–1531) regarded adultery as representing any severe faults in the marriage relationship such as destroying life, endangering life, being mad or crazy, or offending by whorishness (i.e. sleeping around, or being sexually promiscuous). But not all reformers held the view that divorce should be entirely **fault-based**. Some such at **Martin Bucer** (1491–1551) argued that as marriage is based on mutual faith when that faith no longer exists, because the relationship is oppressive, hateful or simply unpleasant then a marriage ceases to exist and divorce should be permitted.

iv Companionate marriage

Two Acts of Parliament in Britain signalled the birth of the modern marriage. In 1857, divorce was made available to all through the law courts (previously it had only been possible for an individual to divorce in England and Wales by an Act of Parliament) and the 1969 **Divorce Reform Act** enabled divorce to be based on the breakdown of the marriage relationship. Up until that time most divorce procedures in Europe had been fault-based. The modern marriage was considered to be a companion relationship and not just a contract or an appropriate place for sex to take place.

We can see this in the Church of England's revision of its Prayer Book service which it had maintained since 1662. A minor revision in 1923 allowed both man and woman in their promises to obey each other but in the *Alternative Service Book* and more recently in the proposals of *Common Worship* (1997) the purposes or aims or marriage are rearranged to place the emphasis on husband–wife relationship. The traditional idea that original sin is conveyed by sex and that marriage is the means of containment of sexual sin has been greatly modified (see Table 5.1). Sex is now celebrated as part of the deeper loving union which is the characteristic of companionate Christian marriage with or without procreation.

Table 5.1: The purpose of marriage in the Church of England	
1662 Prayer Book	**1980 Alternative Service Book**
'It was ordained for the procreation of children, to be brought up in the fear and nurture of the Lord'.	'Marriage is given, that husband and wife might comfort and help each other, living faithfully together in need and in plenty, in sorrow and in joy'
'It was ordained for a remedy against sin, and to avoid fornication'	'It is given, that with delight and tenderness they may know each other in love, and, through the joy of their bodily union, may strengthen union of their hearts and lives'
'It was ordained for mutual society, help, and comfort, that one ought to have of the other, both in prosperity and adversity'	'It is given that they may have children and be blessed in caring for them and bringing them up in accordance with God's will, to his praise and glory'

Sources: *The Book of Common Prayer* (1662)
Alternative Prayer Book (1980)

v Modern husband – wife roles

The gradual shift in expectation for the marriage relationship over the past 100 years may also be one of the reasons for the huge increase in divorce (1 in 2 in USA and 1 in 3 in the UK). It may be that marriage now has to sustain a whole range of personal experiences to a very high level.

A recent Mori poll recorded in the *Daily Mail* (January 1998) indicated that marriage is still believed in by 75% of its sample (2000 people). Some of the other statistics of that survey revealed that:

- 64% believed marriage should be for ever.
- 61% unmarried men wished to marry.
- 37% unmarried women wished to marry.
- 70% of under 25s believed a man or woman should live together with his or her partner before marrying (compared to 53% of married under 45s who have cohabited).
- 67% of under 45s believed it was acceptable to have a child outside marriage
- 28% believed it was better to marry in a church than a registry office.

cited in C Donnellan (editor) *Separation and Divorce* (1999) p 2

2 Catholic marriage and divorce

> **KEY ISSUE**
>
> - Is 'marriage for life' still to be taken literally today?

The principal Roman Catholic teaching on marriage and divorce is that marriage is:

- for the **procreation** of children (and the only place for sex).
- for mutual and life-long faithful **union** of man and woman.
- a **sacrament** (the means by which God's grace is conveyed) which forms a new ontological (a state of being) and **indissoluble** (unbreakable) bond.

There are no grounds for divorce, although it is possible to **separate** or to declare that a marriage never occurred and that it was **null** from the start. Marriage occurs when a man and woman make their promises to each other in front of the priest and two witnesses.

a) Sex and procreation

Marriage is first and foremost a natural state. The *Catechism* states that:

> The vocation to marriage is written in the very nature of man and woman as they came from the hand of the Creator.
>
> *Catechism of the Catholic Church* (1994) p359

Marriage is to be found in all cultures and in a Christian society it is the essence of a healthy family.

Marriage is to be understood not only as a fundamental building block of human relationships but also as a continuation of God's creative love. In the Old Testament book of Genesis, God creates man and woman and then orders a man to leave his own family and in marriage become 'one flesh' through sexual intercourse with his wife (Genesis 2:24). Marriage and sexual intercourse are therefore parallel to God's own loving and creative relationship with the world.

b) Life-long union

Since Vatican 2 (1962–1965) and the encyclical *Gaudium et Spes* (1965) the church has stressed that the purpose of marriage is not only for procreation but also as a union of two people's loving relationship in life. Marriage is both **procreative** (to produce children) and **unitive** (love and companionship) and expresses the love which God showed to humans when he created them.

> God who created man out of love also calls him to love – the fundamental and innate vocation of every human being. For man is created in the image and likeness of God who is himself love.
>
> *Catechism of the Catholic Church* (1994) p359

The physical act of lovemaking through sexual intercourse is therefore the deepest expression of the unitive relationship and at the same time must always be with the intention to procreate. Since Vatican 2 the language of the Church has described marriage as 'conjugal love' and so the family is considered by extension as a '**domestic church**' (*Catechism* p370–371). Both terms put the emphasis on the experience of fellowship, love and grace of the Church to be found in Christian marriage. This is a stark contrast to Augustine's less enthusiastic view of marriage. In other words, the modern Church has shifted the notion of marriage from contract to the notion of **covenant** (a two-way binding relationship) of love.

c) Sacrament and indissolubility

The *Catechism* states that humans live in a fallen world. The original state in which Adam and Eve found themselves was shortly to be replaced by an imperfect state (Genesis 3). It means that no relationship is based on pure love, but is disordered and prone to 'domination, jealousy and conflicts which can escalate into hatred and separation' (*Catechism* p360). Despite this disorder, the Old Testament shows a progressive realisation that marriage was to be monogamous, faithful and loving. Moses permitted divorce because of human sin, but in the New Testament Jesus teaches that divorce was only a temporary state, for now he instructs that 'what therefore God has joined together, let no man put asunder' (Matthew 19:6).

Life-long marriage therefore is possible because as a **sacrament** (an outward and visible sign of words or actions through which God's grace removes sin) pure love is now possible. The presence of Jesus at the Wedding at Cana (John 2:1–11) in which he transformed water into wine, symbolises Christ's presence at every marriage in which God's transforming love removes sin and spiritually unites the couple until death. As distinct from many Protestant views of marriage, the sacramental moment occurs when the couple make their vows in front of the priest at which point they become a new creation and united to God; the marriage is therefore **indissoluble** (it can never be undone). Remarriage is only possible when either husband or wife dies.

d) Annulment

Although by the 13th century the Catholic Church had come to forbid divorce it did not become part of church or **canon law** until the Council of Trent in the 1560s as a reaction to the liberalisation of divorce by the reformers. However, it wasn't until 1917 that the Church fully codified the procedures for divorce and annulment. But its excessive legalisation and lack of pastoral concern prompted more sympathetic procedures in the 1983 Code of Canon Law.

Annulment is a general term which technically means that the Church recognises through its church courts that a marriage contract was null and void from the beginning. Annulment *declares* that a marriage is void, divorce is *effective* by dissolving the marriage bond. The Code of Canon Law recognises two grounds for annulment or the invalidity of the marriage bond.

i Diriment impediment
There are 12 grounds or diriment (i.e. 'nullifying') impediments which determine whether the sacrament of marriage was invalid from the beginning (canons 1083–1095).

- if the man was not at least 16 years old and the woman 14 years old
- if either partner is impotent and cannot have children
- if either is married (unless that marriage has been officially annulled)
- if one of the partners has not been baptised
- if either is bound to the vow of chastity
- if either are in holy orders (as priest for example)
- if the man or woman has been abducted and brought against their will to marriage

- if one of the couple has killed his spouse to marry again
- if they are blood relations (i.e. consanguinity)
- if they are related directly through law (i.e. affinity)
- if the couple are living together after an invalid marriage ceremony
- if adopted children, though unrelated, marry each other.

So, for a Catholic, any marriage which takes place after a civil 'divorce' (i.e. through a non-church law court) constitutes adultery, because the couple are still married in the eyes of the Church and of God. Jesus is recorded to have said in Mark's Gospel:

> Whoever divorces his wife and marries another, commits adultery against her; and if she divorces her husband and marries another, she commits adultery.
>
> Mark 10:11–12

ii Consent

Whereas diriment impediments rest on conclusive evidence and annulment can be granted at speed, far more controversial is proving that one or both of the partners failed to consent to the marriage vows from the beginning. *The Code* sets out three kinds of consent.

- lack of reason: for instance lack of understanding about the obligations of marriage (for children and companionship)
- lack of judgement: for instance that one or the other has deceived the other about the kind of person they are
- lack of psychological ability to carry out the obligations of marriage.

iii Criticisms and defence of annulment

Some have criticised annulment as an easy means of granting divorce without calling it so. In practice the church has always been rigorous about granting annulments. In the medieval church very few annulments were issued. Henry VIII's argument with Pope Clement VII in the 16th century is one of the more famous examples of the difficulty even a monarch had in securing an annulment (and note that technically he did not divorce but had two of his marriages annulled).

Modern Catholics have found the process and grounds for annulment often lacking in human concern. Ladislas Orsy (*The New Dictionary of Theology*, 1990, p21) for instance criticises annulment procedure for its excessive legalism, lack of pastoral and personal concern, and the problems caused in Third World countries where it is not always possible to convene a qualified tribunal.

At the heart of it all is the philosophical problem caused by the retrospective conclusion that a marriage from the beginning was flawed through lack of consent. Can this really be so? And even if this can be demonstrated academically what does it say about the value of the time and effort that may have gone into a marriage. This is a more common criticism especially when viewed by outsiders. The Methodist theologian Richard Jones writes:

> Thus the concept of nullity has been turned into a convenient device for invalidating marriages some of which may for many years have had the true marks and signs of marriage.
>
> R Jones *Groundwork of Christian Ethics* (1984) p127

The *Catechism* is aware of internal and external criticisms of annulment. A Christian marriage after all has to be inspired by the selfless example of Christ and it is the procedures for annulment which give the Church a chance to become involved with a couple's problems. The judicial process may in itself become the means for restoration and the possibility for a new start. The *Catechism* concludes:

> 1 This unequivocal insistence on the indissolubility of the marriage bond may have left some perplexed and could seem to be a demand impossible to realise. However, Jesus has not placed on spouses a burden impossible to bear, or too heavy – heavier than the Law of
> 5 Moses. By coming to restore the original order of creation disturbed by sin, he himself gives the strength and grace to live marriage in the new dimension of the Reign of God.
>
> *Catechism of the Catholic Church* (1994) p362

The Roman Catholic psychiatrist, Jack Dominian (1989), having considered the reasons which lead to marital breakdown, concludes that the notion of nullity, as imperfect as it might seem, goes far further in establishing what a valid marriage actually is. Divorce does not state in quite the same way what constitutes the 'minimum conditions' of marriage, whereas nullity has the job of considering when a marriage is spiritually and psychologically dead. However, Dominian's notion of minimum conditions are not those outlined by the traditional legal impediments stated above but the minimum psychological conditions which constitute a marriage. Dominian's liberal Catholicism is echoed by many others.

> 1 As far as the theological understanding of divorce is concerned, I take the view that the best Christian answer is to back research on the patterns of marital conflict so that we can understand when the minimum conditions are possible. It is no good defending the
> 5 indefensible. If two people cannot undertake the marital relationship, then no marriage exists, however long they may have been living as husband and wife. This is why I prefer the Roman Catholic system, which tries to lay down minimum conditions of what a marriage is and safeguards these.
>
> J Dominian and H Montefiore *God, Sex and Love* (1989) p49

e) Separation

The Church does not use the term divorce but 'separation of the spouses', but there has been a long tradition whereby two kinds of separation are possible. The first dissolved the marriage (in Latin *a vinculo* 'from the bond' of marriage) the second removed marital duties (in Latin *a mensa et thoro* from 'bed and board').

i Remarriage
Canon law recognises that under the Pauline Privilege (canon 1143) a marriage where one or both of the partners was not baptised permits the Church to dissolve the marriage bond. This is not the same as annulment where the marriage bond never existed.

ii Separation without remarriage
The Church acknowledges that marriages can be difficult and time spent apart may be the only humane alternative to living together. In some circumstances a violent partner who threatens the family physically and spiritually means that the full duties of the other partner become impossible. Marriage requires each partner to remain sexually faithful within the sacrament of marriage so a separation means other sexual relationships are illicit. They should in every case, where possible, seek reconciliation.

3 Protestant marriage and divorce

> **KEY ISSUE**
>
> ● If marriage is not a sacrament why is the issue of remarriage so contentious?

a) Lutheranism

Martin Luther's (1483–1546) views on marriage and divorce represent an enormously influential part of the Protestant tradition. It should be noted that Luther did not immediately come to a view on marriage and divorce, but by 1522 he had established certain grounds for divorce. One of the main distinguishing marks of Luther's Protestantism was his rejection of the Catholic teaching that priests should remain celibate. Luther argued that celibacy is not a vocation for everyone but for 'one in several thousands'. By permitting priests to marry Luther placed marriage and celibacy on an equal footing. In his *Babylonian Captivity*, Luther made three important statements which form the basis of a great deal of modern Protestant views of marriage:

● Theologically there is nothing in itself which is distinctive in Christian marriage. It is not a sacrament and does not convey any special grace of God (i.e. it does not remove sin).

● As a phenomenon marriage is not exclusive to Christianity. It is part of human nature for couples to wish to live together; marriage is the term given to the earthly institution which enables the state, through legislation, to assist in the mutual welfare of husband, wife and children.

● Marriage is a mystery or allegory of the relationship between Christ and his Church. The idea that marriage is a sacrament is a mistranslation of the New Testament passage where the Vulgate (or Latin translation) translates the Greek of Ephesians 5:32 'musterion' as 'sacramentum'

The mystery is a profound one, and I am saying that it refers to Christ and the church.

Ephesians 5:32

So 'mystery' in Christian marriage is the unique expression of God's love.

i Sex and marriage

Marriage occurs whenever the man and woman make their promises to each other. Luther argued that marriage is not in this sense a religious obligation and that the Church has no particular control over it; all marriages are valid with or without Church involvement. However, what makes it a Christian marriage is the symbolic moment when the minister gives his blessing. The blessing brings to mind the promises the couple made earlier to each other which now become a binding spiritual covenant in the presence of God. Marriage as an expression of commitment illustrates the central Protestant notion that God's grace is given through faith not the effectiveness of the ceremony itself. The minister's blessing or benediction in the church 'solemnises' the marriage couple's promises and from then on husband and wife dedicate themselves to the spiritual life.

ii Divorce

Divorce could be permitted on grounds of impotence (really a ground for annulment), adultery and refusal to have sex or to live with the other person (desertion). Luther's biblical starting point was based on Matthew 5:32:

But I say to you that every one who divorces his wife, except on the ground of unchastity, makes her an adulteress; and whoever marries a divorced woman commits adultery.

Matthew 5:32 (Revised Standard Version translation)

Luther argues that by committing adultery (which is how he understood the Greek term *'porneia'* or here translated as 'unchastity') the marriage covenant is broken and the bond between man and wife no longer exists. Protestants such as Luther argued that divorce is not contrary to Jesus' command 'let no man put asunder' (Matthew 19:6) because Matthew 5:32 already indicates that God has commanded that divorce is permissible on grounds of adultery.

The Lutheran theologian **Helmut Thielicke** (*The Ethics of Sex* 1964) argues that Jesus' teaching on marriage was to reassert its original purpose in creation, but this did not mean that he totally rejected the Old Testament divorce law; there is still the possibility for a couple to divorce when there is 'hardness of heart' (Mark 10:5). Hardness of heart could be said to occur whenever a husband or wife refuses or rejects the promises made to each other. This does not mean divorce should be easy; it should be considered in extreme cases and then only as the exception to the rule. Thielicke concludes that once a marriage deteriorates beyond repair, then it can be seen that 'it was obviously not God who joined the two together' (*The Ethics of Sex* p168) and the church recognises a divorce through the secular law courts.

iii Remarriage

The problem of remarriage is really a question of guilt. Where divorce has occurred because of fault then remarriage could be seen to condone the sin and to trivialise the church's blessing on marriage. Thielicke writes:

> The sin of remarriage consists rather in the fact that it sanctions another sin, namely, the breaking of the order of creation through *porneia* which destroys marriage.
>
> H Thielicke *The Ethics of Sex* (1964) p182

There can be no general rule, because each case will be dependent on the reasons which led to divorce. Thielicke wonders whether an individual minister will really be able to decide whether a person is sufficiently free from guilt to warrant remarriage. There will also be a natural tendency for the minister's personal involvement and the pressure from others for him to be biased in their favour. Maybe he will lack sufficient objectivity to make a balanced view and for marriage to be blessed by the church again requires even more strenuous effort to consider that the intentions of the couple are in accordance with the Christian lifestyle. However, the principle of remarriage of the innocent party in a divorce is clearly stated by Luther:

> And if he is free, he may take another, just as if his spouse had died.
>
> quoted in H Thielicke *The Ethics of Sex* (1964) p190

b) The Anglican tradition

Throughout the Anglican Church there is diversity of opinion whether marriage is a sacrament, whether divorce is permissible and whether remarriage is possible. However, there is no doubt that marriage for Anglicans (as for other Christians) is significant from other relationships because it is a public declaration of commitment. This is how it is stated in the Church of England's marriage service:

> In marriage husband and wife belong to one another, and they begin a new life together in the community. It is a way of life together that all should honour, and must not be undertaken carelessly, lightly or selfishly, but reverently, responsibly, and after serious thought.

> *Alternative Service Book* (1980) p288

i Is marriage a sacrament?

The Anglican Church follows in the footsteps of Luther and the other reformers by stating that marriage is not a sacrament. The Thirty-nine Articles, which constitute the essence of Anglican belief, make it quite explicit that there are only two Biblical sacraments: baptism and holy Communion (Article 25)

> 1 There are two Sacraments ordained of Christ our Lord in the Gospel, that is to say, Baptism, and the Supper of the Lord. Those five commonly called Sacraments...are not to be counted for Sacraments of the Gospel... for they have not any visible sign or ceremony ordained by
> 5 God.

> *1662 Prayer Book*

Marriage is certainly a holy mystery (the term used in Ephesians 5:32 and misleadingly translated into Latin as *sacramentum*), but the ceremony is not the means of receiving God's grace. Marriage is to be thought of as a binding covenant made between husband and wife (as symbolised in the giving of a ring and exchange of marriage vows) and blessed by the Church. God's grace makes the union a new creation not because of the ceremony itself but through the continuing life-long relationship of love and fidelity. Nevertheless, many Anglicans consider marriage to be a sacrament partly because the power of the marriage service suggests this, and partly because the married life, faithfully lived, signifies that the marriage service is the first moment when God's grace is imparted. This is how Helen Oppenheimer expresses it in her discussion of the power of marriage as a continuous sacramental sign:

> 1 Yet the sacramental character of marriage is a tenacious notion. The solemnity of the marriage service invites the notion that a Christian wedding is a sacrament, even if it is not on a level with a christening or

service of Holy Communion. Even Protestant Christians, when they
5 want a clinching argument against the possibility of divorce, will say as
if it were something we all knew, 'But marriage is a sacrament'. What
they are apt to mean is 'How can we ever break these vows and undo
this joining of hands?' But the theory that marriage is a sacrament is not
particularly about weddings at all.

H Oppenheimer *Marriage* (1990) p58

ii Marriage as a means of grace

In rapidly changing times the notion that marriage is a way of life and
binding covenant allows the church some manoeuvre in
accommodating society's shifting attitudes to sexual relationships and
lifestyles. So, for example, the Church of England's bishops' report
Issues in Human Sexuality (1991) acknowledged that for many people
today the notion that sex can only be experienced within marriage is
unrealistic. There are many types of loving and committed
relationships which 'have some reference... to the institution of
marriage' (p20) and the Church has a pastoral duty to be sensitive to
them. Even so, whilst the Church aims not to condemn, the report
makes it clear that the Christian marriage covenant must be seen as a
far more stable way in which two people can enjoy an effective long-
term, committed relationship.

1 To this complex human situation, which in whole or part constantly
   recurs in history, Christian teaching about marriage offers two things:
   first guidance, based on God's revelation in Scripture and Christian
   experience, as to the way of life within which the full physical
5 expression of our sexuality can best contribute to our own maturity
   and sanctification and that of others; and secondly, a direction in which
   other sexual relationships can and should move, if they are to serve
   more effectually the true fulfilment of those concerned.

Issues in Human Sexuality (1991) p20

By this the bishops mean that Christian marriage is a life of
commitment, sacrifice, loyalty, lack of pride and openness. It is these
sacramental qualities in which God's sustaining grace becomes
possible. The bishops conclude that marriage is the 'means of grace,
making us more like Christ both in ourselves and in our dealings with
the world around us' (*Issues in Human Sexuality* p21).

iii Divorce and the law

In 1951, Mrs Eirene White introduced a Bill proposing that where a
couple had lived apart for seven years with no prospect of
reconciliation, a divorce should be granted without having to prove
offence of either party. In 1956 a Royal Commission was set up to
consider new grounds for divorces and as a result coined the new

principle of **irretrievable breakdown**. The churches' reactions were for the most part strongly opposed to anything which undermined the sanctity of marriage. But in 1964 Archbishop Ramsey put together a group to consider the law of divorce. It must be noted that their consideration was not to establish church principles but what should be considered best for all members of society.

In 1966, the Commision published *Putting Asunder: a Divorce Law for Contemporary Society,* which was widely admired for its clarity and bold proposals. It recommended that the old accusatorial procedure based on fault (often where there was none, or where it had been invented in order to secure a divorce) and nominating the 'innocent' and 'guilty' party should be replaced with a more humane non-judgemental system. The law should be based on the single notion that all divorce should be determined on grounds of 'breakdown with inquest'. This went much further than either Mrs White or the Royal Commission had anticipated.

The result was a compromise whereby some of the old 'grounds' were now recast and used to define the single ground of breakdown on evidence of one or more of the following: adultery, unreasonable behaviour and desertion. The Archbishop was critical of the new 'grounds' which he considered would make 'marriage more attractive to an adventurer or adventuress' (A Winnett *The Church and Divorce* p100). The subsequent rise in the divorce rate of 25,000 in 1970 before the Act became law from 119,000 in 1972 and 121,000 in 1975 proved the archbishop's fears to have been partially right.

It should not be imagined, however, that *Putting Asunder* expresses the official view of the Church now or then. Whilst those who hold liberal Bucer-like views of marriage (see page 79 above) consider a marriage to have ended once the bond of love is destroyed, the indissolubilist maintains that the vows at marriage are binding for life. The advice of the report hinged on what it considered to be practical for society as a whole, rather than what should be the Christian ideal.

The bishops' report *Issues in Human Sexuality* concedes that divorce is tragic, though sometimes necessary. The bishops try to strike the middle path. On the one hand they accept that the Matthean exception (and Pauline Privilege) permits the practice of divorce (see pages 101–102 below), but on the other hand it is clear that the thrust of Jesus' teaching was based on the principle that marriage is God's primary purpose for men and women in the created order.

iv Remarriage

At present there is no one view held by member churches in the Anglican communion. The situation is summarised here by the statement issued at the 1998 Lambeth Conference (the ten-yearly meeting of all the Anglican bishops throughout the world). The Conference distinguished three 'ways' of sexual behaviour.

- Way 1: 'Faithful and righteous family life, based on love and mutuality' as expressed in marriage.
- Way 2: Sinful ways which fall short: promiscuity (both heterosexual and homosexual), adultery, prostitution, child pornography, active paedophilia, bestiality and sadomasochism.
- Way 3: Less than complete expressions of the Christian way. These would include some forms of African traditional marriage (polygamy for example) and faithful cohabitation.

A third example of Way 3 which concerns many parts of the Anglican Communion is the remarriage of divorced people. Earlier this century it would have been accepted by most Anglicans that remarriage after divorce is a serious impediment to Christian living, and a complete impediment for the ordained ministry. There are parts of the Anglican Communion where this remains the normative position. For some Anglicans remarriage after divorce does not represent Way 1. Nevertheless in an increasing number of churches, remarriage of some divorced people is recognised and blessed in the Church both for the laity and for those who are ordained. This remains a divisive issue, but there is a growing recognition that remarriage after divorce is not to be identified with Way 2.

1998 Lambeth Conference

In practice remarriage is left to the conscience of the individual priest or minister. Some feel that someone who was the wronged party should not be punished again by refusing them remarriage. Others argue that Christianity is a religion of forgiveness and should allow remarriage where there can seen to be genuine remorse and repentance for past actions. Moves to have some standard procedure about remarriage in the Church have failed to win a consensus, although a recent Church of England report *Marriage in Church after Divorce* (January 2000) recommends that church law should be amended to recognise that in some circumstances a couple should be formally released from their marriage vows and free to remarry in church.

Both the bishops' report and the Anglican churches throughout the world acknowledge that marriage is having to compete against a range of other socially acceptable relationships. The question of whether cohabitation for homosexual as well as heterosexual couples is morally acceptable in the Christian tradition is one of the most important challenges to all Christian denominations (see Chapters 4 and 6).

However, whereas there are clearly many good religious reasons why marriage is desirable there are far less obvious non-religious moral reasons why marriage today should be considered the most satisfactory means of conducting an adult sexual relationship.

4 Non-religious marriage and divorce

> **KEY ISSUE**
>
> ● Is marriage necessary for non-religious people?

Marriage is still considered by many people to be a socially desirable way on which to base their relationships. But without the religious enforcement of sacrament or divine command, what are the non-religious reasons for marriage? Some Marxists, for example, have considered marriage in idealistic terms to be an important expression of a transformed society based only if men and women can be complete equals. Other humanist thinkers suggest that marriage really only becomes significant when children are born and society is obliged to give them legal protection through the institution of marriage.

a) Marxism

In their initial analysis of society **Frederick Engels (1820–1895)** and **Karl Marx (1818–1883)** considered marriage to be a symptom of all that was wrong in a class-ridden, capitalistic and hierarchical society. Marriage they argued is all to do with ownership and possession. On one level this can be seen at the literal level where marriage is the means by which one family buys into the wealth of another. We can see this today. People tend to marry those of the same class, religious, ethnic and political outlook. A 'good marriage' is still considered in some quarters to be advantageous in terms of business transactions or material gain. Marriage in this sense promotes the existing economic social structure.

i Marriage is exploitative ownership

At another level marriage is to do with **ownership** and possession of the man over the woman (or possibly the other way round). At the heart of Marx's and Engels' critique of society was the notion that the ownership of property was a major way in which the bourgeoisie (the classes who own the means of production) could maintain power and exploit the working classes or proletariat (who own nothing).

Marriage, Engels argued, in its present form, is a bourgeois institution which perpetuates the false moral values of the bourgeoisie at the expense of full and loving human relationships. Monogamous marriage, Engels argues, in a capitalist society is not liberation as Christians believe, but a form of slavery or 'prostitution' (as he calls it) of women which, because of its unsatisfactory nature, has constantly led to widespread adultery and infidelity in search of real relationships. So, Engels turned the Christian argument upside down: marriage is the cause of sin not its containment! He argues that:

- Monogamous marriage suits the bourgeois classes because it legitimises the right to inheritance of money and property.
- Monogamous marriage is based on conflict of husband and wife; 'it exhibits in miniature the same oppositions and contradictions as those in which society has been moving'.
- All examples of real love (in literature for instance) in the past have always been outside marriage because marriage restricts proper relationships.
- Marriage is impossible in a capitalist culture. Real marriage of equals based on love can only occur when it is removed from any presence of ownership and exploitation of men over women, or women over men.

ii Marriage of equals

Engels clearly expresses why many today have abandoned marriage due to its traditional inequalities, the constraint it places on full relationships and its perpetuation of sexual ethics which are regarded as out of date. Even so, we must not forget that despite his criticisms Engels' utopian vision of society (when there is complete economic equality) envisages marriage as the only place for a full loving relationship between men and women. But if this state of affairs is economically impossible, does this mean that marriage is inevitably bound to fail in today's capitalist society?

1   The modern individual family is founded on the open or concealed domestic slavery of the wife...

Then it will be plain that the first condition for the liberation of the wife is to bring the whole female sex back into public industry, and that this
5   in turn demands that the characteristic of the monogamous family as the economic unit of society be abolished.

We are now approaching a social revolution in which the economic foundations of monogamy as they have existed hitherto will disappear just as surely as those of its complement – prostitution...

10 Monogamy arose from the concentration of considerable wealth in the hands of a single individual – a man – and from the need to bequeath this wealth to the children of that man and of no other. For this purpose, the monogamy of the woman was required, not that of the man, so this monogamy of the woman did not in any way interfere with
15 open or concealed polygamy on the part of the man. But by transforming by far the greater portion, at any rate, of permanent, heritable wealth—the means of production—into social property, the coming social revolution will reduce to a minimum all this anxiety about bequeathing and inheriting. Having arisen from economic causes, will
20 monogamy then disappear when these causes disappear?

One might answer, not without reason: far from disappearing, it will, on the contrary, be realised completely... Prostitution disappears; monogamy, instead of collapsing, at last becomes a reality – also for men.

F Engels *The Origin of the Family, Private Property, and the State* (1884)
Chapter 2 part 4

iii Engels and Feminism
The Marxist view as expressed by Engels has been very influential:

● For many social reconstructionist feminists marriage is to be avoided because of its patriarchal formation and basis on male values, ownership and exploitation of women.
● Marxist analysis has helped fuel a transformation of marriage from ownership to liberated companionate relationships based on mutual trust and economic independence (although its effects on the family have been less positive – see page 169).

b) Humanism and modern marriage

Modern humanism argues that all human institutions should be based on reason not superstition or religion. The Marxist view of marriage outlined above is one such form of humanism but based on a very particular view of society. Other humanists, such as John Stuart Mill (1806–1873) have based their reasoning on what makes for a happy and contented life. The **utilitarian** principle tends to lead to a **libertarian** view of marriage and divorce which places the responsibility on the couple to decide on the scope and commitment of their relationship. The function of the law is not to make moral judgement but to ensure that the rights and requests of the couple are fairly administered at divorce.

i Open marriage
Some people have argued that providing both husband and wife are absolutely honest in their relationship with one another, then each may have a sexual relationship with someone outside marriage. Those who advocate this kind of marriage argue that rationally it is better for sexual needs to be satisfied in an open and honest way with the permission of the other. But humans do not always function on a rational basis. For example, in the film *Indecent Proposal* (1993) the husband allows his wife to sleep for one night with a man in exchange for a million dollars. This may seem objectively to make good utilitarian sense; but as time goes by he becomes increasingly consumed with jealousy and doubt about his wife's motives and commitment to him. Eventually the marriage breaks down. In the same way 'open marriage' may simply be a contradiction in terms and impossible to sustain.

ii Marriage for children

Quite often couples who have cohabited choose to marry when they wish to have children. Even in 1929 the philosopher and humanist **Bertrand Russell (1872–1970)** argued that the only really serious consequences of a sexual relationship which necessitated marriage was to provide children with a stable environment. Furthermore, once children are involved the relationship can no longer be considered a private affair but becomes a public concern. Marriage, as a legal institution, provides some insurance that the children will have two parents to bring them up and care for them.

> 1   In a rational ethic, marriage would not count as such in the absence of
> children. A sterile marriage should be easily dissoluble, for it is through
> children alone that sexual relations become of importance to society,
> and worthy to be taken seriously by a legal institution. (p125)… I think
> 5   that all sex relations which do not involve children should be regarded
> as a purely private affair, and that if a man and a woman choose to live
> together without having children, that should be no one's business but
> their own (p132).

> B Russell *Marriage and Morals* (1929) p125 and p132

iii Serial monogamy

> 1   I think uninhibited civilised people, whether men or women, are
> generally, polygamous in their instincts. They may fall deeply in love and
> be for some years entirely absorbed in one person, but sooner or later
> sexual familiarity dulls the edge of passion, and then they begin to look
> 5   elsewhere for a revival of the old thrill.

> B Russell *Marriage and Morals* (1929) p122

Despite the increase in divorce rates there is continuing evidence to indicate that marriage is still regarded by many as highly desirable. Liberal divorce laws are essential if the principle of personal autonomy and happiness is to be the basis of a liberal society. Russell and other humanists recognise that a marriage is based on equality and shared interests, 'I believe marriage to be the best and most important relation that can exist between two human beings' (*Marriage and Morals* p115).

Now that much of the stigma and taboo has been lost from divorce it has left couples free to form and reform relationships creatively and in accord with their needs. This has not reduced the significance of marriage but allowed for the realities of human nature, the fact that people live longer, are more independent and have higher expectations in marriage than before. The acceptance of serial monogamy from the humanist position does not necessarily undermine marriage but accepts that the happiness of the individual today needs freedom to change and adapt to new circumstances in life.

But is serial monogamy socially desirable? What effects does it have on children and the family? Recent debate about the family has focused on the utilitarian consequences of divorce. This is a complex issue (see pages 172–173) but Russell's views illustrate what many regard to be an unacceptably strong emphasis on adult individual choice at the expense of children and the institution of the family.

5 Marriage and divorce law

a) A brief history of marriage and divorce law

- From 1547 divorce was only possible in each case by a **special Act of Parliament**. The Church of England was divided whether divorce *a vinculo* should be permitted.
- In 1670 an Act permitted Lord Roos to remarry whilst his former wife was alive. Despite opposition from the Church this set a precedent which was the basis for the 1857 Act. Over 187 years 317 private Acts (and divorces) were passed.
- **1753 Lord Hardwicke's Marriage Act** made it obligatory for all marriages (except Jews and Quakers) in England and Wales to be conducted before a Church of England minister and two witnesses with the compulsory consent of parents for minors (i.e. below the age of 21). Clandestine marriages were outlawed.
- **1857 Matrimonial Causes Act** allowed civil courts to dissolve marriages *a vinculo* on grounds of adultery. The bill compelled a clergyman to allow a divorced innocent party to remarry using his church building.
- **1937 Matrimonial Causes Act** ('The Herbert Act') included additional grounds of divorce: three years' desertion, cruelty and prolonged incurable insanity. Annulment also included wilful non-consummation of marriage. A wife could also divorce a husband for rape, sodomy or bestiality. In 1957 a more conservative Church passed an Act of Convocation resolution refusing all remarriages in church – although it permitted 'private prayers' to be said by the clergy for a couple who had been divorced in the civil courts.
- **1969 Divorce Reform Act** was based partially on the principle suggested by the Church of England's report *Putting Asunder* of 'irretrievable breakdown'. Subsequent amendments to the law have allowed proceedings to take place without both parties appearing in court.

b) Legal arrangements for divorce in England and Wales

The following is an example of the legal arrangements for divorce in England and Wales under the present laws.

Irretrievable breakdown has to be demonstrated in one or more of the following five categories:

1. Adultery
2. Unreasonable behaviour
3. Desertion (two years continuously)
4. Two years separation (with the consent for divorce of both parties)
5. Five years continuous separation (without consent for divorce from one party)

Filing for divorce can only take place after one year of marriage. The procedure follows in this way:

● Either husband or wife files for divorce to the court. They are known as the **petitioner**.
● The court sends the petition on to the other party who in law is known as the **respondent**.
● The petitioner then sends a sworn statement (or **affidavit**) that the grounds for divorce are true.
● The respondent may wish to dispute the divorce petition. If they do not contend the petition they may wish to make it clear that they do not admit any fault.
● The court issues the **decree nisi**. At this stage the court may make any arrangements for children and other financial arrangements.
● After six weeks and one day, the petitioner applies for the **decree absolute**. Once this is issued the marriage is legally ended.

6 Marriage and the Bible

> **KEY ISSUE**
>
> ● How might a critical study of the Bible help to reconsider the purpose and value of marriage and divorce today?

The primary consideration for many Christians has been the interpretation of New Testament where marriage is explicitly discussed. We have already seen that there exists today an important distinction between those who see marriage as being indissoluble and those who allow for divorce as a last resort. In this section we shall only consider the scholarly debate surrounding these biblical passages, other discussions about the nature of marriage as a sacrament or 'mystical union' must be seen to be part of the wider discussion touched on above.

a) Old Testament

i Marriage
There are no specific marriage ceremonies mentioned in the Old Testament or Hebrew Bible, although a feast or dinner seems to have accompanied the moment when a couple were considered to be married. The Old Testament reflects an evolving view of marriage from the polygamy of the patriarchs to the monogamy of the first century CE. Polygamy, for instance, is expressly forbidden by the Essene community at Qumran (*Temple Scroll* 56:18–19). The following points characterise the ideas of marriage which form the background to the New Testament and 1st century rabbinic Judaism.

- **The father's power.** Before marriage a girl was considered to be the property of the father and under his control. For instance, the criticism made of King David when he slept with Bethsheba, Uriah's wife, was not in the first instance that he had committed adultery, but that he had stolen Uriah's lawful property (2 Samuel 12:1–4). (See Countryman *Dirt, Greed and Sex* chapter 8 for detailed discussion of the meaning of property ownership in ancient Israel.)
- **Bride price.** The first stage of marriage was a contract between the two families often ratified or confirmed by a gift from the husband to be to the father of his fiancée (Genesis 34:12, Exodus 22:16–17).
- **Betrothal.** At the next stage, between the ages of 12 and 12½, the girl left her father and became a member of her husband's household and was treated as a 'wife'. During this period of betrothal, which lasted for about a year, separation was only possible through divorce.
- **Marriage.** Only when the couple had had sexual intercourse together and 'become one flesh' (the Hebrew word used here is to cleave meaning to 'glue together') were they considered fully husband and wife. As a wife she was different from a servant in that her marriage contract gave rights of property possession. The children which followed confirmed the success of the marriage and the future of the family (e.g. Psalm 127:3–5). Marriage in other words was a process from leaving her father to cleaving with her husband (Genesis 1:27) to the birth of children.
- **Duties.** The role of the wife was essentially in the home and to her husband. Proverbs 31:10–31 sings the praises of the wife who manages the affairs of the household and is responsible for the education of the children. So marriage wasn't always just considered to be contract and property ownership. Tobit 8:6 talks of the social advantages and mutual happiness which a good marriage brings.

ii Divorce
Divorce was the right only of the husband since his wife was now under his power and not her father's. However, if he raped or forced sex on an unbetrothed virgin not only had he to pay the bride price

and marry her, but he lost his right to divorce (Deuteronomy 22:28–29). Likewise if he accused his wife of not being a virgin at marriage and this proved false he also lost his right to divorce (Deuteronomy 22:13–19).

● **Fidelity.** The Old Testament tradition stressed fidelity in marriage – the prophet Micah condemns the man who divorces his wife in old age in favour of a younger one (Micah 2:14–16 and see also Sirach 7:26). Divorce therefore acts as a means by which a wife who is socially embarrassing (Sirach 25:26) may be dismissed.

● **The grounds for divorce.** Countryman comments, 'The Torah did not legislate directly on the matter of divorce, but simply alluded to it in passing as something which a man might do if he found in his wife "anything improper" (*Dirt Greed and Sex* p173). Deuteronomy 24:1 says:

> When a man takes a wife and marries her, if then she finds no favour in his eyes because he has found some indecency in her, and he writes her a bill of divorce and puts it in her hand and sends her out of his house, and she departs out of his house.

The key words here are *erwat dabar* in Hebrew or as the Septuagint (or Greek translation of the Old Testament) translates *porneia*. There has been endless debate what this means. By the 1st century CE the rabbis had formed various interpretations, though none had rejected divorce. The followers of the rabbi Shammai for instance took it to mean adultery – a serious infringement of the ten commandments. But the school of rabbi Hillel, on the other hand, was far more liberal in its interpretation and it is their view which Jeremias reckons was prevalent in the 1st century CE (see *Jerusalem in the Time of Jesus* p370). The *Mishnah* (2nd century CE record of rabbinical debate) says:

> The school of Shammai says, 'A man cannot divorce his wife unless she has been unfaithful because the Torah says, "she finds no favour in his eyes because he has found some indecency in her."' But the school of Hillel says, 'He may divorce her even if she failed to cook a meal properly for him because as the Torah says 'He has found some indecency in her'.
>
> *Mishnah Gittin* 9:10

In practice a husband had to provide financial support for his wife on divorce as laid down in the marriage contract; this may well have acted as a deterrent from hasty action.

b) New Testament

We have to remember that by the time Jesus' words were recorded in the gospels they had already been shaped according to the practices and needs of the communities for whom the evangelists were writing. This does not necessarily mean that we do not have Jesus' actual words, but what sayings we have are selected, commented upon and presented from a different point of view from the one Jesus may have originally addressed. Even so most scholars agree that whereas there is no reason to suppose that Jesus did not accept the contemporary Jewish practices and ceremonies of marriage, where he differs is in the nature of marriage and divorce.

i Marriage

The nature of marriage arises from a discussion of divorce (Mark 10:1–9). Jesus' response follows a rabbinic device by looking at the order of texts – as he asks them what was written 'in the beginning' (10:6) meaning from the book of Genesis (1:27). The answer is that marriage is the union of man and woman and is part of the creation. So it follows that divorce was given later (in the book of Deuteronomy 24:1) because humans could not live up to God's ideal. Clearly Genesis expresses God's original and pure intention that marriage is a new creation which no human can uncreate. Whatever this passage may imply about divorce it is clear that the uniqueness of Jesus' teaching is that he has elevated marriage from mere property exchange to a unique aspect of God's creation. The author of the letter to the Ephesians provides us with an extended commentary on his understanding of Jesus' teaching. He begins by quoting Genesis 1:27 and then depicts marriage in spiritual and mystical terms of the love which Christ expresses to his church.

> This mystery is a profound one, and I am saying that it refers to Christ and the church; however, let each one of you love his wife as himself, and let the wife see that she respects her husband.
>
> Ephesians 5:32–33

The gospels' presentation of Jesus does not explicitly mention love as the characteristic of Christian marriage, but for the writer of Ephesians it is clear that he understood Jesus to have meant that the marriage covenant is to be expressed as a bond of love. He had presumably reflected on the essence of Jesus' teaching and applied it directly to marriage.

ii Divorce

So did Jesus' words in Mark 10:1–10 (and also Matthew 19:3–9) permit divorce?

● Some argue that Jesus' intention was not necessarily to abandon the Law of Moses on divorce but to express in the strongest possible terms what marriage should be. As we have seen there was already a powerful tradition amongst the later prophets and other Jewish writers that marriage was about mutual respect and could not be abandoned with ease. In other words, Jesus leaves the question of divorce for humans to decide.

- Jesus would have understood that marriage would be destroyed by adultery – indeed in Matthew's version the phrase 'And I say to you: whoever divorces his wife, except for unchastity, and marries another, commits adultery' (Matthew 19:9) is closer to what Jesus intended. This is the so-called Matthean exception and would be consistent with the line taken by the school of Shammai.

- But amongst scholars there is some disagreement about what *porneia* means. 'Unchastity' or *porneia* in Greek can refer to a number of illicit sexual relationships. Some argue that Matthew took *porneia* to mean that the wife was not a virgin at marriage and that this would invalidate the marriage bond. Others feel that Matthew has added the words from his Jewish background because adultery would have meant automatic divorce. Others take *porneia* to mean consistent infidelity – not just adultery but blatant promiscuity and disregard for the Christian notion of marriage. This would be much closer to Paul's privilege to allow divorce when one clearly had no intention of keeping to the Christian ideal. The addition of the exception may be a softening of Jesus' point of view but it does not necessarily lessen Jesus' special emphasis on marriage as a new creation and the state to which Christians should aspire.

- Both Paul (1 Corinthians 7:12–15) and Mark (10:10–12) allow for divorce. In Mark the setting is 'in the house' – perhaps as an indication that this is Mark's own additional teaching and Paul explicitly states that his teaching is 'not from the Lord'. Mark's text is ambiguous. He says that if either man or woman remarries after divorce then the relationship is adulterous. This could be taken in the Pauline sense that divorce is permissible in a mixed marriage (of Christian and non-Christian) but no remarriage is possible.

- On the other hand, Paul states that divorce was not permitted by Jesus. In which case Mark could be emphasising the indissolubility of marriage with a powerful metaphor suggesting that all divorce is equivalent to adultery. What he describes is a Roman situation where men and women could have the option of a civil divorce so Mark is emphatically stating that this is not an option for his community. If we remember that in the Old Testament the punishment for adultery was death (Deuteronomy 22:22–24 and see John 8:5), then we can see that divorce is considered so bad that it should be treated as equivalent to a capital punishment offence. So, as Anthony Harvey concludes:

An act (divorce) which was legal, but which under certain circumstances attracted moral disapproval, is described by Jesus as one of the most serious crimes: it will be called (or equivalent to) adultery.

A Harvey *Strenuous Commands* (1996) p86

Answering structured and essay questions

Questions

1. **a)** What are the principal reasons for marriage?
    b) 'Marriage is still the best environment for the nurture of children'. Discuss.

2. **a)** Outline the reasons why Engels considered marriage to be a form of property exploitation.
    b) To what extent do you think Engels' views about marriage are still true today?

3. Assess the theological and social reasons why annulment is preferable to divorce.

4. 'An open marriage is much more likely to work in the long term than a traditional one'. Discuss.

5. Discuss how the Christian churches should develop the institution of marriage into the 21st century.

Essay skills

This chapter has shown the centrality of Christian marriage in Western society. It is important that you are able to refer to the different stages of its development and understand how the question of divorce was central to the debates in the Reformation. The debate continues. The three 'ends' or 'goods' of marriage receive different emphasis at various times. Compare the Christian 'ends' with non-Christian – how different are they? The question of marriage is not a trivial one and distinguishes those who consider that marriage cannot be dissolved from those who look to the quality of relationships (companionate marriage). All these notions have serious implications for social policy, children and society today. Consider the reasons for divorce: are expectations too high? Have certain forms of feminism created new roles for men and women which traditional marriage cannot sustain? Engels' essay, although deeply flawed, continues to provide a useful atheistic alternative by which to judge theological and utilitarian ideas of marriage.

Summary of secular and theological reasons for marriage

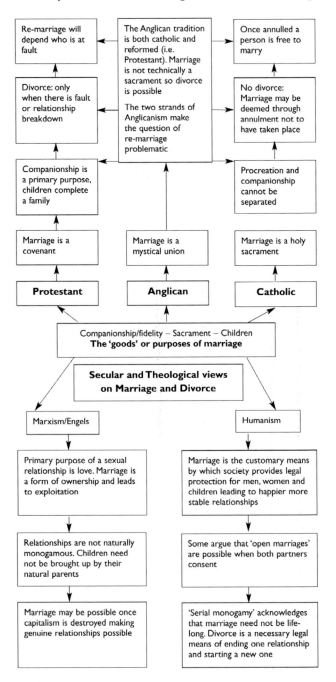

6 Cohabitation: conditional and unconditional love

KEYWORDS

betrothal – the formal stage before marriage which is considered to be almost as binding as marriage itself, usually without sexual intercourse

CARE – Christian Action Research and Education argues for the social desirability of marriage as opposed to cohabitation.

categorical imperative – Kant's description of what constitutes universal moral duty

cohabitation – a man and woman living together within a sexual union without the formality of legal marriage

cohabitation contract – a contract or agreement drawn up to formalise a couple's responsibilities to each other and arrangements if they separate

common law marriage – a partnership of man and woman judged to be equivalent to marriage without them having been through a legal ceremony. Not part of English law (except in Scotland)

creation ordinance – the statement in Genesis 2:24 in which marriage is described as the process of leaving home, cleaving to one's partner, bonding and forming a family. It describes a universal sequence

hedonic calculus – Bentham's criteria which determine how to calculate happiness

living in sin – a pejorative term which regards cohabitation as morally wrong and against God's will

1 Public or private relationships?

1 I am living with my partner (cohabiting it is now known) and we have a daughter. I have never been happier and my daughter is happy too. My partner came from a broken marriage where he was in a relationship for a short time before marrying. We have been together seven years
5 and have never seen the need to 'commit' to each other by marriage – it wouldn't change anything apart from my surname and an extra piece of paper to keep!

from a BBC online survey, February, 1999

A revolution in personal relationships over the past 30 years has been the rise and near universal acceptance in the West of cohabitation. Cohabitation may be defined as:

> A co-resident man and woman, living together within a sexual union, without that union being formalised by a legal marriage.
>
> Office of Population, Census and Surveys

Whereas in the past cohabitation was considered to be shameful, a taboo and to be 'living in sin' the mood is now such that what people choose to do in private is their own affair. Put more formally, a liberal principle argues that providing there is no harm inflicted on others, if a couple choose to live together in a sexual relationship (with or without children) there are no specific moral reasons why they should not do so. Cohabitation has burgeoned throughout the Western world: in 1996, 46% of babies in Norway were born out of wedlock, in 1991, 50% of all Americans in their twenties and thirties had cohabited outside marriage, and in Canada 10% of couples live together without being married. British trends are set out in Table 6.1.

Table 6.1: Cohabitation trends and attitudes in Great Britain

- The proportion of all non-married women aged 18–49 who were cohabiting in Great Britain in 1981 has doubled to 25% in 1996–1997.
- Women aged 25 to 34 are the most likely to cohabit (31% of all cohabiting women), a third higher than those aged 18 to 24.
- The proportion of never-married women who were cohabiting increased from 9 per cent in 1981 to 27% in 1996–1997.
- Men aged 25 to 34 are most likely to cohabit, but less so than women (19% of all cohabiting men).
- For both men and women, those whose marriages have ended in divorce are the most likely to cohabit, although cohabiting is more common among divorced men than divorced women.
- Between 1991 to 1997 the most common reason for cohabitation ending for women was for the marriage of partners (15% of all women cohabiting).
- Of all those women who started cohabitations each year, over six in ten were single, that is never married.
- A third of all those aged over 60 thought cohabitation was wrong compared with less than a tenth of those under 30.
- The number of first-time marriages was 185,000 in 1996 half the number in the peak year of 1970.

Source: *Social Trends* 29, 1999, p 47

The question is whether the increase in cohabitation is morally and socially desirable. Table 6.1 suggests that among young adults the majority have few moral objections to cohabitation. This may account for the decrease of first-time marriages but nevertheless marriage is still regarded by the majority as the ideal way in which to conduct their relationships (see page 81) 75% in that survey. Cohabitation not only poses particular problems for Christian churches where marriage represents the heart of family and social life, but also for legal reforms. If marriage is a public declaration how can the law protect the interests of each party in what is essentially a private affair?

At different stages in history the following 'ends' or 'goods' of marriage have been emphasised to a lesser or greater extent.

- **Fidelity**: Marriage is considered to be permanent or, at very least, long term and sexually excludes others. It defines a relationship which can be recognised by family, society and law. Older views of marriage considered marriage to be the means by which to regulate sex and 'contain sin'.
- **Companionship**: Marriage is for mutual companionship (the 'unitive') of both partners, sexually and socially. A legal system can ensure the rights and interests of each partner in that relationship.
- **Procreation**: Marriage is for the procreation of children into a stable environment in which they are to be nurtured so as to become responsible members of society. The law can ensure that parents carry out their parental duties.

Philosophically cohabitation gives an important insight into what people currently consider to be the essential ingredients of morality: long- and short-term consequences, pleasure, commitment, duty, responsibilities and love. The one element which most clearly distinguishes cohabitation from marriage is commitment.

2 Types of cohabitation

There are generally recognised to be three kinds of cohabitation relationships (or 'living together').

a) Casual cohabitation

The least formal cohabitation relationship is characterised by the lack of long-term commitment. It might begin with a casual sexual relationship and develop so that by living together both partners share a common sexual and social life. Often for symbolic and practical reasons one partner may keep his or her flat/house as a sign of independence. Casual cohabitation, unlike marriage, is private, informal and, by its very nature, transitory. Fifty per cent of all cohabitation relationships belong to this category and last on average no longer than two years.

b) Trial marriage cohabitation

A survey in 1994 found that 54% of those interviewed regarded living together before marriage to be important if not essential. Many argue that before taking such a serious step as marriage both partners should be sure that they are compatible to ensure that the marriage will last. This form of cohabitation by definition is not an ideal state and suggests that it is at best conditional, private, short-term, and open-ended. Quite often if children are born the additional responsibility may act as a catalyst for marriage so as to give them the benefits of a more stable and long-term environment.

c) Substitute marriage cohabitation

Increasingly there are those who never marry and have no intention of marrying. The reasons for this are complex, but the conscious decision might be:

- observation that marriage as an institution has failed through very high divorce rates (almost 50% in the USA and UK)
- marriage is more to do with pleasing others and not oneself
- marriage assumes an unrealistic level of long-term commitment
- marriage is based on traditional and outmoded views of gender roles
- marriage is often perceived to be unnecessarily expensive and bureaucratic
- marriage may be a religious commitment but for the agnostic or atheist there are no absolute moral reasons which make cohabitation immoral
- marriage places too much emphasis on the legalistic and not on the quality of the relationship
- relationships should be open ended enough to be able to change in time and circumstance without the trauma or stigma of divorce
- marriage is a heterosexual institution and inappropriate for homosexual lifestyles.

3 Utilitarian arguments

> **KEY ISSUE**
>
> - If marriage is just a 'piece of paper' then does cohabitation as an alternative bring more or less happiness?

The reasons for cohabitation set out above suggest many of the positive criteria why modern relationships flourish without the need for traditional marriage. Humanist utilitarian arguments question whether relationships need to be long-term or for life or indeed exclusive provided that people are happy. Is it necessary to have a ceremony or public promise to make a relationship any more committed?

Statistical empirical evidence gathered by some organisations to suggest that on utilitarian grounds cohabitation does not make people happier in the long term. Often their agendas are set by traditional morality or conservative Christian claims, but as CARE (Christian Action Research and Education) argues, those who are opting for a cohabitation relationship should at least be aware of the negative effects of cohabitation.

In his utilitarian **hedonic calculus** Jeremy Bentham stated that: 'To a person considered by himself, the value of pleasure or pain considered by itself, will be greater or lesser according to':

its intensity
its duration
its certainty or uncertainty
its propinquity (whether it is close at hand or far off)
its fecundity (i.e. likelihood of producing more pain or more pleasure)
its purity (its likelihood of not producing more happiness or pain)
its extent (that is its effects on others)

> J Bentham *An Introduction to the Principles of Morals and Legislation*
> (1788) Chapter 4

a) The pain of breakdown

The breakdown of any relationship is painful but does cohabitation make this any easier to handle? Philippa Taylor argues in her publication for CARE, *For Better For Worse* (1998) that as the certainty of breakdown in cohabitation is six times greater than that of marriage, it is necessarily less satisfactory than the intention in marriage to develop a long-term, stable relationship.

On the other hand, it might be argued that break up is far less intense in cohabitation: it is an inevitable characteristic of a less formal arrangement and can proceed without the trauma of divorce courts and the stigma of a failed marriage.

b) Fear of rejection

Taylor argues that cohabitation, unlike marriage, has inevitably to function with uncertainty. In Bentham's calculus, happiness is also to be reckoned in terms of the likelihood of experiencing more of the same (fecundity). But is this possible without the formality of marriage where partners promise not to desert each other in sickness or for someone else. Some have complained that where a relationship has broken down they have not received the same kind of social support and legal help which a divorcing couple are given. The ease of entering cohabitation has to be matched by the ease of separation.

c) Health problems

Taylor (*For Better for Worse* pp28–33) cites much recent research that illustrates the potential increase in health risks of cohabitation as opposed to marriage. These, in Benthamite terms, are probably less likely for the young cohabitee than for those later in life where the prospect of finding another partner is more likely than later in life. In the calculus this has to be considered as an issue of propinquity and duration – a short-term or long-term issue. Marriage is designed to cope with the long-term 'till death do us part'. For instance, Taylor cites research which indicates that married men generally live a more settled and secure life and earn 10% more than cohabiting men (see *Male Wages and Living Arrangements* Davies and Peronaci, 1997 cited in Taylor *For Better for Worse* p 23).

Cohabitation is therefore considered a health risk on the following grounds:

- There is higher rate of alcoholism.
- Higher smoking amongst cohabiting pregnant women and potential health threats to the foetus
- There is a 8–17% increase in death rate for those with cancer who are cohabitees than for married couples.
- There is a higher incidence of single male suicides than married men.
- Abortion is 10.2% amongst cohabiting women compared to 2.6% of married women. Abortion is not without its contingent side-effects: guilt, risk of sterilisation and depression.
- Higher incidence of venereal disease: 6.3% cohabiting women visit clinics compared to 1.1% married women.

d) Violence

Domestic violence is equally likely to occur in marriage as in cohabitation. However, Taylor cites research which indicates that cohabiting women are twice as likely to experience domestic violence than married women: 35% compared to 25% married women. In the United States, the Department of Justice reported that between 1979 and 1987 65% of violence against single/cohabiting women was by a boyfriend or ex-husband as opposed to 9% by husbands in married relationships (see G Stanton *Why Marriage Matters* 1997 p63). What this may suggest is that many rush into cohabitation without finding out more about their partner. Furthermore, many argue that this reinforces the idea that cohabitation as 'trial marriage' is meaningless. For if couples need to find out more about each other before cohabitation, then cohabitation is no more of a trial than marriage itself.

e) Cost to the many

The final element of Bentham's calculus is that pain and pleasure should be judged and legislated for according to its extent or effect on the many. Taylor argues that cohabitation costs the nation not only in direct financial terms but also in the emotional breakdown of families. In addition, the perceived attractiveness of cohabitation is also a contributory factor to family breakdown.

- Cohabitation is responsible for the increase in single parent families (a quarter to a half of all families are single parents), which is considered to weaken the institution of the traditional family.
- Cohabitation has reduced responsible fatherhood.
- Cohabitation costs the tax payer in increased social security benefit pay-outs.
- Separation (and divorce) increases the cost to the tax payer through legal aid court costs.
- Cohabitation does not provide children with a certain and stable future.

4 Unconditional and conditional duty

> **KEY ISSUE**
>
> - Does commitment in a sexual relationship necessarily mean an intention to be with someone for life?

Whatever considerations the utilitarian might contribute to the pragmatic debates about cohabitation in terms of outcome (pain and pleasure) a weakness of such a view is that it fails to consider the more important and fundamental moral values of trust, love, promise keeping and commitment. These are often theological values, but they need not be. **Immanuel Kant (1724–1804)** argued that the moral law which Christians support need not have its origins in God's will but in the rational application of human will.

a) Kant's two kinds of duty

Kant distinguishes between two kinds of duty. **Contingent duty** (sometimes referred to as the hypothetical imperative) merely informs us what we should do in certain circumstances. If I want to catch the train to go to London, then I must set off from home now. But contingent duty or obligation is utterly different when it comes to dealing with people. Moral duty or obligations cannot be conditional (if...then...) but unconditional. Kant states the **categorical imperative** in various forms, but in essence what he claims is that morality is not based on desire but the good will. What I will for myself

I must will for all. In this way moral behaviour is to be consistent, universal and above all treats other humans not as means to an end but as ends in themselves. Happy and fulfilled lives only result when a person is secure in the knowledge that their values are upheld by others.

b) Critique of casual cohabitation

Casual cohabitation is least likely to satisfy Kant's criterion to be morally acceptable. It is by its very nature short-term, conditional and contingent (there are no long-term unconditional promises). However, those who participate in casual cohabitation might respond that if both parties know they are using each other (for sex for instance) then no one is hurt, and furthermore they would whole-heartedly recommend it to others. This simply begs the question. From a Kantian perspective the hurt caused is a result of treating each other as a means to an end and not as a person. It is wrong because the conditions are based on personal desire and not on what is good for the other.

c) Critique of trial marriage cohabitation

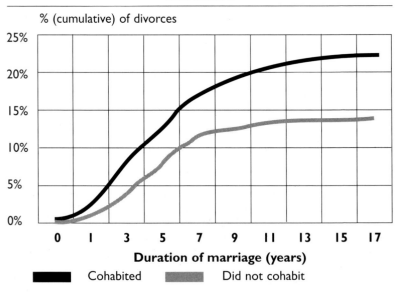

Table 6.2 Marriages ending in divorce or separation by premarital cohabitation

Source: *Population Trends* no 68 cited in
Cohabitation or Marriage? by D Flanagan and T Williams (1997) p16

The Kantian critique is more conclusively illustrated in the case of trial marriage cohabitation. There is statistical evidence of what is sometimes referred to as the **cohabitation effect**. This is thought to demonstrate that those who cohabit before marriage are far more likely to divorce once they do marry than those who do not live together before marriage (see Table 6.2).

A CARE report *Cohabitation or Marriage?* (1997) argues the following:

1 Data from the General Household Survey shows that a couple who cohabit before marriage are, on average, twice as likely to divorce as a couple who do not cohabit before marriage. For example, among women between 40 and 50 who married when they were in their early

5 twenties (20–24) and who cohabited before marriage, 39% were divorced compared to 21% of those who did not. Taking all age groups, the ratio of divorce between couples who premaritally cohabited and couples who did not cohabit, is 1.8 to 1, showing an 80% greater likelihood of divorce among those who cohabited before marriage.

10 Information collected by the General Household Survey allows divorce rates by duration of marriage to be estimated for couples in their first marriage. From this data the probability of a marriage ending in divorce or separation can be calculated for both those who cohabited premaritally and those who did not…Amongst those

15 divorced, the prevalence of cohabiting before a second marriage has always been higher than before a first marriage. The older the man or woman, the greater the proportion who cohabit premaritally before their second marriage. The idea that premarital cohabitation reduces the likelihood of an unhappy marriage is false.

D Flanagan and T Williams *Cohabitation or Marriage?* (1997) pp15–16

Whilst the conclusion of the authors is too sweeping the evidence does highlight the weakness of those who choose cohabitation because they are not yet ready to be committed to marriage. Kant's important distinction between contingent and categorical duty is also one between a relationship based on conditions and one based on long-term duty. This is not necessarily making the case for marriage – although the promises or vows made at marriage suggest the unconditional nature of marriage. There is no reason why a couple should not make promises to each other unconditionally yet choose not to make these public. Equally we could argue that marriage is conditional. Fault based divorce or the idea of irretrievable breakdown presupposes that duties can be broken depending on circumstances.

Even so, there is a moral contradiction in the 'trial' element of this kind of relationship. If a couple choose to cohabit fully intending to marry then there is no trial at all. Marriage merely marks the public and legal moment and recognition of what is to all intents and purposes already a 'marriage'. If, on the other hand, it is truly a trial then the notion of marriage is qualitatively different. A couple then have to move from the conditional (cohabitation) to the unconditional (marriage) and it may be this experience which is the subsequent cause of marital and relationship breakdown; so from a Kantian perspective it suggests that trial marriage is no more moral than casual cohabitation.

d) Critique of cohabitation as substitute marriage

There are many reasons why people choose to cohabit rather than marry.

i Excluded groups
The first category may include those who would like to marry but are prohibited from doing so for religious, cultural or legal reasons.

- A couple may choose to cohabit because their families refuse to let them marry outside their religion or class.
- A husband or wife may refuse the other a divorce for religious reasons. Legally the separating person is unable to remarry and so chooses to cohabit.
- A gay or lesbian person is not recognised under existing law to have the right to marriage (see page 54) and so has to opt to cohabit.

From the perspective of each of these couples their intentions are considered to be equivalent to marriage promises. This does not make their relationship licit (lawful) from the point of view of society or a religion – indeed depending on the definition of marriage, a gay couple could never fulfil the duties of marriage (i.e. through lack of procreation), or a person who cohabits whilst technically married to another commits adultery and may place him or herself outside the communion of their church tradition (see pages 87–88). But what all these cases have in common is the lack of public recognition which prohibits them from becoming formally married.

Thus whilst intentions might satisfy Kant's categorical imperative, each couple would also know that it could not consistently be applied universally to be the equivalent of marriage.

ii Ideological cohabitation
The second category are those who consciously reject marriage on ideological grounds. Those who argue for marriage are, as we have seen from the conservative pressure group CARE, keen to promote traditional values and social structures. Often their agenda is based on another ideology which defines marriage in narrow terms.

Social reconstruction feminists (see pages 24–27), for instance, argue that marriage is essentially a patriarchal institution which is more interested in ownership and control of women by men and an insistence on the role of man as bread winner than liberated and genuine human relationships. The argument was forcefully made by Frederick Engels (1820–1895) in the 19th century – and although he did envisage a time when marriage might be possible it would be marriage along very different lines from the marriage of his day. To a great extent the economic conditions that Marxist feminists have campaigned for have become part of Western culture. A woman no longer needs to marry for economic survival; a woman need not be a homemaker or even a child bearer. The traditional ends or goods of marriage are therefore unnecessary and detrimental for a liberated and satisfactory relationship (see pages 28–30 for a fuller argument).

The alternative to marriage offered by some feminists differs only in so far as it replaces some of the traditional ends or goods of marriage and traditional gender roles. The Kantian critique need have no specific criticism where a relationship is committed and based on mutual obligations which are non-exploitative. It is the final point, which for all practical purposes, questions whether cohabitation as a private affair is desirable. Whereas the social institution of marriage, as it has evolved, protects the rights and freedom of both partners, a cohabiting couple has no special protection other than individual rights. However, many countries now have evolved systems of **registered partnerships**, which offer couples the same kind of rights and protection of the law. For example, in Sweden and Denmark cohabitation is the norm, and marriage is marginalised.

Some couples settle on a **cohabitation contract** or agreement setting out the terms and obligations of their relationship to suit their needs. It is difficult to see how this is an improvement on marriage and could certainly appear to be more restrictive than the obligations of marriage. Above all, it appears to turn a relationship into a set of contractual conditions rather than the more general promises of marriage. Critics of cohabitation frequently point out how individualistic and egocentric it can be. Perversely some forms of cohabitation appear to be closer to an older view of marriage as contract, which radical feminists, especially, have tried to avoid.

Finally there is a widespread view that marriage is 'just a piece of paper'. Whilst clearly this is wrong from a legal point of view, it is significant in what it tells us about how many see their relationships. Marriage is frequently considered to be an expensive, over–emotional occasion. Although this an erroneous understanding of marriage, many philosophers consider that it reflects the state of late modern culture where relationships of all kinds are far more fluid, open-ended and experimental. The consequences for the family and society are profound (see Chapter 8).

5 Rights and the law

The problem which cohabitation faces in law is that because it is by nature a private affair it cannot have the protection of the law unless the partnership is recognised. One view might be that expressed by CARE:

1   There are regular calls to give cohabitation the same status as marriage. However, these ignore the fact that cohabitees have deliberately (if temporarily) rejected the ties of marriage – they have chosen cohabitation because it is different from marriage, because it is easier
5   to walk into and out of and because it appears to give the individual freedom from the responsibilities and restrictions of marriage.

P Taylor *For Better for Worse* (1998) p9

Table 6.3 The legal situation in England and Wales for Cohabitation

- Cohabitation agreements or contracts might have little weight in law since they lack 'valuable consideration' – especially when it comes to the consideration of matters that cannot be valued, such as children or lack of security (if a woman had carried a more traditional role as mother and homemaker).
- If a woman dies intestate (that is without making a will) her money does not pass automatically to her children. Her children would have to prove that they are her children to become eligible for inheritance.
- A woman who separates from her partner cannot sue him for maintenance as if she were married.
- A woman is not entitled to a widow's pension on the death of her partner.
- A partner has no legal right of ownership or occupation to a house lived in by both partners, unless his or her name appears jointly on the tenancy or conveyance. Where children are involved the court has the power to order a transfer tenancy to both partners.
- If a partner dies without making a will, unlike marriage, the surviving partner has no legal right to the deceased's estate. A cohabitant can make a claim but must show that he or she has been dependent and maintained by the deceased partner.

Marriage provides a range of rights and responsibilities which can only be matched if each cohabitation relationship chooses to regulate their relationship through individual contracts.

6 Theological considerations

> **KEY ISSUE**
>
> ● Do all Christians consider that cohabitation is 'living in sin'?

Ideally the Christian church prefers a situation where a couple who intend to live together make their intentions public (engagement) and then marry by making their covenant promises to one another with the blessing of the church. There is, nevertheless, a wide difference of opinion about what constitutes marriage – whether it is an indissoluble sacrament, whether a ceremony is necessary or significant, whether remarriage is permissible. Marriage from the Christian perspective means a permanent, life-long union between man and woman. It is symbolised by the biblical term 'to cleave' (Genesis 1:27) meaning to 'cling' and as Jesus expressed it, 'to become one flesh' (Mark 10:8) in a life-long monogamous relationship and not in any temporary fashion.

So, cohabitation presents the church with a problem. Increasingly young Christians cohabit before marriage and cohabiting couples who choose to marry in a church may already have started a family. We shall consider three possible and overlapping theological responses: the traditionalist anti-cohabitation; the liberal inclusivist; and the progressive.

a) Traditionalist anti-cohabitation

The starting point held by conservative evangelical and Roman Catholic Christians is that **pre-marital sex** (sex before marriage) is wrong and constitutes the sin of **fornication**.

i Virginity and sex

In the Old Testament virginity was a prerequisite of marriage (Deuteronomy 22:18–19), and if a man found that his wife was not a virgin then he was released from his marriage bond and she would be stoned to death (Deuteronomy 22:20–21). A man who seduced a virgin (Exodus 22:16-17) was forced to pay the bride price and marry her. The notion is carried on into the New Testament. In 1 Corinthians 7:28, Paul assumes that virginity should be the normal state before marriage. It is a view supported by other writers in the New Testament. The author of the Hebrews 13:4 writes:

> Let marriage be held in honour among all, and let the marriage bed be undefiled; for God will judge the immoral and adulterous.
>
> Hebrews 13:4

Sex in Christian terms expresses the covenant relationship of 'one flesh', which is marriage. Sex before marriage assumes that sex is being practised for reasons other than that of life-long fidelity.

Traditional Christian teaching places the emphasis first on relationship and considers too much is made of sex. Edward Pratt argues the case:

1   Sex is a good servant but a terrible master. Only later do Jack and Jill
    discover that they have not really got much in common – and split. Also
    dissatisfaction with sex may itself be the reason, as couples have
    discovered they are not achieving the unrealistic goal of perpetual sexual
5   bliss which is held up as a target by some opinion-formers today.

Living in Sin? St Simon's Church (1994) p12

ii Love and responsibility

Marriage is the process whereby a couple invest in each other. From the start, marriage assumes the sacrifice of self-interest for one's husband or wife and then children. It means a disciplined life of responsibility. Christian love or 'agape' is illustrated by the self-sacrifice of Christ for others. Cohabitation rarely encompasses any of these Christian qualities. Those who are restrained and wait to be married before sex also learn to be disciplined within marriage and faithful to their partner. Furthermore, for Christian traditions which base their moral reasoning on natural law cohabitation is illicit because any sexual relationship which firstly does not intend to produce children and secondly lacks commitment cannot achieve the purpose of sexual intercourse. This view is expressed in the Pope's encyclical *Familiaris Consortio* (1981 paragraphs 80–81) and in the *Catechism*:

1   The expression 'free union', is fallacious: what can 'union' mean when the
    partners make no commitment to one another, each exhibiting a lack of
    trust in the other, in himself, or in the future? The expression covers a
    number of different situations: concubinage, rejection of marriage as
5   such, or inability to make long-term commitments. All these situations
    offend against the dignity of marriage; they destroy the very idea of the
    family; they weaken the sense of fidelity. They are contrary to moral law.

Catechism of the Catholic Church (1994) p512

iii Parents and cohabiting children

Christian parents therefore face a difficult problem when their own children choose to cohabit. How should they regard the couple? For traditionalists this is a painful dilemma. If they treat the couple as a couple then they would be seen to condone or approve of a relationship which they actually regard as sinful. On the other hand, the example of Christ was not to shun sinners but to mix with them and by example set the standard of behaviour demanded by the Kingdom of God. Many parents are acutely aware that if they are too critical they risk alienating themselves from their son or daughter, or if judgmental they are not exercising Christian compassion and forgiveness.

iv Cohabitation and the need to repent

The marriage ceremony in traditionalist's terms is a powerful and symbolic moment when the seriousness of the vows expressed mark the moment when marriage truly begins. Words and actions combine to reinforce the moment. For many, the outward symbols and the presence of the priest suggest that marriage is a sacrament, a moment when God's grace establishes a new relationship between husband and wife 'so they become a new creation'. So, how should a priest or minister prepare those who wish to marry if they are already cohabiting and may already have children?

Many traditionalists, such as Edward Pratt (*Living In Sin?* pp21–22), argue that it is entirely appropriate that a Christian couple who have cohabited should repent. This should be through word and deed – Pratt advises living apart and abstaining from sex until after the marriage. And for those who have children he argues that the minister should refer to their repentance in the wedding service. Finally those who refuse to repent should be advised to marry in a registry office.

b) Liberal inclusivist

The radical alternative to the Christian traditionalists are those who place less emphasis on the ceremony of marriage and more on the quality of the relationship itself. Whilst it may be true that many cohabitation relationships are sinful, egocentric and exploitative it doesn't follow that they all are. Each relationship has to be judged on its own merits.

i Sexual fidelity and sin

Virginity is not in itself a prerequisite for a successful marriage. What virginity symbolises is faithfulness, commitment and purity of intention. In 1 Thessalonians 4:3–8, Paul speaks of sexual control. Sexual faithfulness may be equally expressed in cohabitation as in marriage; the view of the traditionalist on sexual abstinence perversely makes disproportionate fuss about sex. Liberal Christian theology argues that the view of the body as the source for sin through sex belongs to a very different view of the self (see pages 11–12 above). Sexual drives are seen to be part of the instinctive natural self, not sin; the body is no longer a vessel purified by a good soul. This suggests that the *telos* or purpose of sex is not primarily to procreate, as the natural law tradition argues, but principally an expression of committed love.

The liberal theologian differs from the traditional view presented by St Paul and St Augustine who argued that marriage was for the containment of sin (concupiscence) (see pages 77–78). A relationship can only be judged sinful if it is exploitative, abusive, selfish – attributes that St Paul himself described as antitheses to Christian love (1 Corinthians 13). The Christian view of marriage has always depended on the free consent of the two persons and that may be equally so of those who cohabit faithfully as those who choose formal recognition.

ii Marriage is not a ceremony
The liberal position argues that marriage as an institution has been a convenient way in which to give a couple the legal support and rights to ensure that their relationship has every chance of success. Marriage though, is not the ceremony itself, as beautiful and as helpful as that moment might be, but the promises made from one partner to another in the presence of God. The blessing of the Church as the reformers (see page 87) argued, may only help the couple to recognise the seriousness of their promises – the Old Testament, for example, does not prescribe any ceremony (see page 99) and the requirement for promises to be said in front of a priest was only introduced in the West at the Council of Trent in 1563.

iii Cohabitation can be Christian
Not all cohabitation relationships can be Christian. Casual cohabitation, like casual sex, cannot fulfil the degree of commitment which 'cleaving' suggests. But an unconditional cohabitation based on Christian agape-love, though unconventional, is nevertheless a Christian 'marriage' in all but name. Whilst present laws exist it may be expedient for a couple to marry to ensure the full benefit of rights for each of the couple and their children. A priest or minister need only look at the quality of their relationship to judge whether the blessing of the church confirms what has already been established.

c) Progressive

A major weakness of the liberal Christian view is that it underestimates the significance of the marriage ceremony and the blessing given by the Church. Marriage in Christian terms is also a social commitment, whereas the liberal view tends only to stress the personal. A progressive argument is less severe on judgement than the traditionalist but nevertheless regards cohabitation to be less than best.

i Marriage as a process

The tendency in recent times is to see marriage occurring at a particular moment in church. The increase in cohabitation and especially trial marriage cohabitation draws attention to both the Biblical and social reality that marriage was in the past a process. The biblical process is consistently presented as the 'leaving-cleaving-bonding'. Some have called this the **creation ordinance** as it not only describes the process outlined in Genesis 2:24 but is also the universal picture of what happens in marriage the world over. Jeremy Collingwood (an Anglican priest and barrister) argues:

> 1   This means that where the creation ordinance is fulfilled there is a valid marriage in the view of Scripture. Even though marriage may be regulated to comply with the particular legal norms of any one society, its validity is not compromised in the biblical perspective. A man and a
> 5   woman who fulfil the requirements of the creation ordinance are man and wife in the eyes of God.

> J Collingwood *Common Law Marriage* (1994) p8

The criticism therefore of the traditionalist view is that it places too much weight on the marriage ceremony itself. A couple may already have embarked on 'marriage' by living together (leaving and cleaving). Indeed, in the more recent past marriage was understood to be a series of increasingly binding moments often marked finally by a feast but not necessarily so. It was only in 1753 that English civil law required a ceremony to mark the final stage or public 'bond', and even then many working-class people chose not to formalise their cohabitation but to live as common law husband and wife.

ii Betrothal and Biblical marriage

Some theologians have argued for the need to reinstate the more ancient and biblical practice of betrothal. They argue that certain forms of cohabitation (e.g. trial marriage) in effect reintroduce the stage before marriage itself. But although betrothal indeed marked the period before marriage until the marriage settlement was given it differs from cohabitation to the degree in which it was legally binding on the couple to marry. Even in 18th-century England, where betrothal amongst the plebian and middle classes was a private promise (sometimes signified with a broken shilling) in the eyes of the community it was considered to have the status of marriage. Betrothal usually took place before sexual intercourse, though not always (Hitchcock, *English Sexualities 1700–1800* p33), but it was certainly not unusual for the bride to be pregnant at the church service. A marriage ceremony (whether in church or by ancient symbolic custom) only marked one moment in the process.

But a comparison with the past does not entirely work. Cohabitation today assumes a sexual relationship which does not contract the couple to each other. An understanding of the past may help to re-think cohabitation as part of an ancient, though modified, process to marriage.

iii Common law marriage

Collingwood suggests that both the church and the state should reintroduce the notion of **common law marriage**. This is when a couple has lived as husband and wife in a committed relationship the law should give them the full rights of marriage and the church should acknowledge that their relationship is in accordance with the creation ordinance and regard their relationship as a Biblical marriage.

This poses a series of practical problems. What length of time establishes whether the couple are living as man and wife? When and how should the law recognise their status? In short, it is the public aspect of conventional marriage which distinguishes it from the provisional nature of cohabitation. The weakness of all arguments of this kind is why a couple should wish to register their relationship when there is already the existing system of registry marriage. Collingwood though offers another argument of **presumption after the fact**. This is where a couple can demonstrate their relationship has been that of husband and wife and that they should be regarded to have contracted common law marriage and with all the rights and protection of legal marriage.

The Church, though, should still teach that marriage is the best environment for a relationship to flourish. It gives a definite signal to family and friends that a couple wish to be considered as a couple and for children to know that their parents' relationship is not provisional but permanent.

iv Sin and pastoral concern

Collingwood criticises the suggestion made by Pratt that a cohabiting couple should be required to repent and live apart. He argues that all couples need some repentence – why should this particular aspect of their lives be singled out? For example, if only 10% of brides are virgins should every wedding ceremony have a moment when bride and groom confess past acts of fornication? For Collingwood and others it is sufficient that a couple now wish to fulfil the creation ordinance 'we have no right to lay upon them the obligation to live apart' (*Common Law Marriage* p11).

The progressive view therefore attempts to take into account the increasingly commonplace existence of cohabitation. The Church has a pastoral role to encourage people to take on the responsibilities and commitment which are the intrinsic characteristics of Christian marriage whilst refraining from assuming it can judge a relationship merely because it has not gone through the traditional process. The role of parents and ministers must be to encourage marriage as the better way and support the means for legal reforms to make marriage generally less formidable than it seems to have become.

Answering structured and essay questions

Questions

1. **a)** Explain how cohabitation is different from marriage.
   b) 'Why marry when it is easier to cohabit' Discuss.

2. **a)** Why do some people claim that the idea of 'trial marriage' is a contradiction in terms?
   b) 'Cohabitation is selfish and sinful' Discuss.

3. 'A relationship based on conditions cannot be morally ideal but it is realistic' Discuss.
4. To what extent is cohabitation a moral or pastoral issue?
5. Which exploits a relationship more: marriage or cohabitation? Consider both theological and philosophical arguments in your answer.

Essay skills

Although cohabitation is often considered by contrasting it with marriage, all the issues here are essentially about adult sexual relationships. The first distinction you will want to make in most of your answers is between the private and informal nature of cohabitation and the formal/public function of marriage. Be clear that by 'formal' it need not refer to a church wedding, or gathering, but simply a public recognition of a relationship. Consider this from Kant's non-religious distinction between conditional and unconditional duty or the Christian notion of unconditional love. But do people want long-term relationships? Do they want their relationship to be recognised by society? What advantages does a registered partnership have over marriage? You may wish to include here the criticisms of feminists and homosexuals (see Chapters 3 and 4) that marriage is too patriarchal and exclusive, or that cohabitation is freer and more satisfactory than marriage. But also consider the empirical data and the so-called 'cohabitation effect'. Finally, evaluate whether cohabitation is theologically really only a pastoral issue or one which needs to reconsider the nature of traditional marriage and sexual morality.

Summary diagram

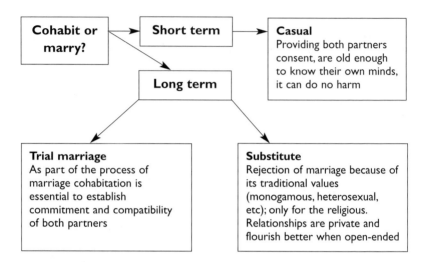

Ethical considerations

Is trial marriage really possible if commitment is conditional? What does a relationship gain through formal, public and legal recognition? Should all sexual relationships be informal?

Kant

The most important consideration is that people are never treated as means but ends in themselves and that suggests that relationships should intend unconditional commitment. This may or may not satify a cohabitation arrangement

Utilitarian

Some empirical evidence suggests that cohabitation does not lead to greater happiness. Problems caused to children, greater abuse of women by men, etc. Lack of certainty. On the other hand, long-term commitment can stifle a relationship

Christian

Traditional views consider all sexual relations outside marriage as fornication. Progressive views argue that cohabitation may be part of the marriage process. Liberals consider that if two people are committed to each other that is what is meant by marriage

7 Reproduction

1 Reproductive rights and responsibilities

There often seems to be an essential unfairness about having and wanting children. Some children are conceived when the parents do not desire a child and the parents then have to decide whether to proceed with the pregnancy. Other couples, on the other hand, would give almost anything to have a child of their own, but for one reason or another are unable to do so. They might then consider whether they should use artificial or assisted reproductive means to help them have a child.

There is also for some an essential moral contradiction in planning a family. Whereas it is considered to be morally responsible not to bring an unwanted child into the world it is also equally regarded by many to be a right to have a child. Today, as never before, these issues are particularly acute because the technologies and methods exist to assist and limit reproduction that give couples a range of choices unthinkable before the mid 20th century. Technology offers hope to those who in the past would have simply accepted that they could not have children. Equally technology has given men and women considerable autonomy to control their reproductive powers whilst enjoying their sexual relationships.

All these considerations touch on some contentious areas of human rights:

- Do a couple have a right to a child by artificial means such as **surrogacy** or **artificial insemination** or **in vitro fertilisation**?
- Do a couple have a right and a duty to control their reproductive powers by using **contraception**?
- Does a woman have a right to terminate an unwanted pregnancy by **abortion** or an **abortifacient** (or a chemical means of causing an abortion)?
- What rights does the foetus have? Is it right to use technology involving **human cloning** or experiments on human foetuses to produce 'perfect' babies?

The moral issues consider whether all such rights are accompanied by the appropriate responsibility; in almost every case the object of those responsibilities must be the child itself. The speed of change often means that the law has not provided sufficient safeguards against the unscrupulous and the vulnerable. In all these related areas emotions are enormously powerful. However, moral, theological and legal reflection must provide a rational basis for all such provisions.

2 Surrogacy

KEY ISSUE

● How does one define the idea of a 'mother' morally and legally?

Surrogacy is a general term used to describe the situation where a woman bears a child for another couple. Some dispute whether 'surrogacy' is an appropriate term. A surrogate mother is the one who adopts a child as her own; a mother who bears a child (whether or not it is genetically related to her) is the mother. This is an important and central distinction. The 'host' or surrogate mother undergoes all the emotions and psychological changes that accompany a pregnancy and it is these experiences which have to be taken into account. If it were possible to hire an incubator or lease a womb independently of the person, then there would be no sense in which the machine or disembodied womb could be considered a mother. The key moral and legal question is to what degree a contract can be binding on the surrogate mother to relinquish the child when it is born.

a) Surrogacy and law

Surrogacy poses questions about what is meant by being a parent. This can be seen in the range of terms used:

● **Social or intended parents** are those who initiate or commission the surrogacy and bring the child up as their own.
● **Genetic parents** are those who provide sperm and egg.
● **Surrogate mother**, or host mother, who bears the child. It is an ambiguous term. If, for instance, the 'surrogate' provides genetic material she is also the 'biological mother' and the social mother is strictly the surrogate. Legally the surrogate mother is the child's mother not the intended mother.

The issues are further complicated by the type of surrogacy used:

● **Partial surrogacy** occurs when the surrogate or host mother provides her egg which is fertilised either *in vitro* and placed through artificial insemination into the womb or she is artificially inseminated by the intended father's sperm. Only in very rare cases would sexual intercourse take place.
● **Full surrogacy** occurs when the intended parents provide egg and sperm. In some cases a donor (either egg or sperm) may be used. The fertilised gamete is placed into the host's womb.
● **Commercial surrogacy** refers to arrangements whereby a woman is contracted and paid to be a surrogate mother and to deliver a baby to the intended parents. In many countries commercial surrogacy is illegal.

● **Voluntary** or **altruistic surrogacy** refers to a surrogacy arrangement where the surrogate mother voluntarily offers to bear a child for another couple but not for commercial gain. Her motives could be out of love (a sister's love for her sister or brother) or charity (a Christian concern for a childless couple to have a family) or self-fulfilment (the sensation of having a baby).

The law in England and Wales is governed in this way:

Table 7.1 Surrogacy and the Law

1985 Surrogacy Act: it is illegal to arrange, agree about or take part in a commercial arrangement for surrogacy. Altruistic surrogacy is not illegal, i.e. when there is no financial gain. Payment is considered to have taken place if there is the involvement of a third party or if the surrogate expects a payment to be made. It is also illegal to advertise for a surrogate mother. Reasonable payment for loss of earnings, treatment costs, child care, etc. are permitted. The British Medical Association defined this in 1996 to be £7,000–£10,000.

1990 Human Fertilisation and Embryology Act: amended the 1985 Act so that surrogacy arrangements cannot be enforced by law. The intended parents may become the legal parents of the child, but until that time the child is legally the surrogate mother's. A parental order must be arranged six weeks after and six months within the birth of the child (even if both intended parents are also the genetic parents). The child must be living with the intended parents in the UK, must be over 18 and married. The surrogate mother must be in agreement. The birth certificate will be altered, but at 18 the child will be able to obtain a copy of the original certificate which will contain the name of the surrogate mother.

If the surrogate has supplied her egg to be fertilised she is to be treated as a donor and the same screening procedures apply to her as with any donor and controlled by the licensing authority.

---

b) The case of 'Baby M'

The most important and influential surrogacy case took place in 1986. The case of 'Baby M' (as it was referred to in the courts) is significant because of the legislation which took place afterwards concerning surrogacy contracts and also because of the continued moral issues which it raises.

The essential facts of the case are as follows (see Pence *Classic Cases In Medical Ethics* pp 121–132):

● Elizabeth and William Stern are both well educated and well-to-do physicians living in New Jersey (USA).
● Elizabeth thought she should not have a child as she claimed to have the symptoms of multiple sclerosis and having a baby would exacerbate the condition.

- In 1985 they chose Mary Beth Whitehead (husband Richard) to be a surrogate because she looked similar to Elizabeth. Both the Whiteheads are lower income earners and he is an alcoholic. The surrogacy is commercial (she agreed to the $10,000 contract) and partial (she provided the egg and William the sperm). Richard initially had misgivings.
- During the pregnancy, however, Mary Beth thinks of the baby as 'hers'. She fails at first to have an amniocentesis test despite the condition of the contract. Later she does and learns of the sex of the foetus. She fails to divulge the information to the Sterns.
- She tells her own children that she doesn't want to 'sell their sister'.
- Reluctantly just before the birth she signed the paternity papers that would give the baby to the Sterns.
- Baby M is born on 27 March 1986. Richard is registered by Mary Beth as the father. First Mary Beth allows the Sterns to have the baby then says she feels suicidal at the thought of giving up the baby and the Sterns allow her to take the baby home for a week. Then she refused to give up the baby and the baby is hidden.
- The Sterns take the case to court.
- In a taped phone call Mary Beth said to William:

    'I took care of myself the whole 9 months. I didn't take any drugs. I didn't drink alcohol. I ate good. And that's the only reason that she's healthy, Bill. Only because of me, because of me… I gave her life. I had the right during the whole pregnancy to terminate, didn't I Bill?'
    'It was your body.'
    'That's right. It was my body, and now you're telling me I have no right.'

- Mary Beth falls ill and whilst she is in hospital the baby is found and returned to the Sterns to look after as a temporary custody measure.
- At the trial (January 1987) the case centred on Mary Beth's character: she was considered to be a liar and had accused William Stern of sexually abusing her own children. The judge concluded that commercial surrogacy contracts were not illegal and the baby should be legally considered to belong to the Sterns. The judge was accused of bias. Many feminists supported Mary Beth: 'A one night stand in a dish doesn't make a man a father' and that surrogacy was a form of 'reproductive prostitution'.
- On 3 February 1988, the New Jersey Supreme Court reversed the initial decision on appeal and ruled that surrogacy contracts were illegal and constituted a form of baby selling. The Sterns were allowed to keep the baby but Elizabeth could not adopt her and Mary Beth's status was confirmed as the legal and natural mother.

c) Ethical issues of surrogacy

Before the 'Baby M' case there had been hundreds of surrogacy births in the USA, only four of which had resulted in disputes. Gregory Pence wonders whether one case which went wrong should be responsible for the subsequent alteration to the law. However, what the case did was to highlight a practice that the public was largely unaware of. The reactions from churches, feminist groups and many others allowed the ethical issues that had not had the opportunity to be fully aired before to be brought out into the open.

i Autonomy and contracts

Firstly, we should consider, along with the liberal utilitarian, why there should be any particular problem. If three possibly four adults (including the surrogate's husband or partner) wish to enter freely into a contract to produce a child what possible harm can there be? This is the view held, for instance, by Michael Kinsley, editor of the American publication *New Republic* (1987):

1   The basic moral case for contract law, indeed for capitalism itself, rests on the voluntary nature of exchange. Commercial trade is good for all parties involved, or else they wouldn't engage in it. And in the vast majority of commercial transactions – including the vast majority of

5   surrogate-motherhood contracts – the deal goes through with no problem, suggesting that both parties do indeed consider themselves better off.

    M Kinsley quoted by G Pence in *Classic Cases In Medical Ethics* (1995) p139

However, it is the question of *harm* which is central to many of the debates about surrogacy. The liberal position does no more than beg the question. Can a contract really be held to be binding if it violates certain rights or when one party is being unwittingly exploited?

ii Motherhood

The issue of surrogacy (along with IVF see page 143 below) questions what it means to be a mother. Is it a necessity for a child to have a mother who is genetically related to him or her? There is no consistent answer here. On the one hand, as in the case of 'Baby M', many feminist groups argued that Mary Beth, the surrogate, should be considered the real mother – she had after all not only provided the genetic material but nurtured the child from conception. Motherhood might then be considered to be more than simply providing an egg but the intimate, psychological, possibly spiritual, process of giving the foetus/baby its first formative experiences. Supposing, though, Baby M had been conceived using full surrogacy; would the lack of genetic contribution by Mary Beth have made any difference to the motherhood argument?

    There are parallel arguments in cases where parents adopt a child. It is far from clear whether a mother is any less of a mother if she has not nurtured the child in the womb, or whether, from the child's point of view, his mother is less of a mother because he is not genetically related to her. There is some evidence to indicate that children do have a strong desire to know where they have come from; this cannot be entirely divorced from a child's own sense of identity and relationship with his or her parents.

iii The good parent

The case of 'Baby M' highlighted the emotive issue of what constitutes a good parent. Those who accused the judge of bias suggested that he had been swayed by the Sterns' middle class background and had decided from the start that Mary Beth was not a good parent. And yet, as far as the law is concerned in England and Wales, those intended parents entering on a voluntary surrogacy agreement have no guarantee that they will be able to adopt the child, if they are not married or considered to be unsuitable prospective parents. Whereas any couple can have a child through natural means whatever their politics, racial mix, or social behaviour, those wishing to adopt have to pass rigorous interviews to show that they will be 'good parents'. It is not only a grey area in law but morally highly subjective.

The alternative would be to screen all potential parents before they started a family. But besides the impracticalities, such a gross invasion of the human right to exercise our personal liberties would undermine some of the fundamentals of a liberal democracy. However, the cases are not entirely parallel; it is because surrogacy is an *artificial* process involving a form of public contract that the law is able to impose some regulations for the general good which might well entail determining what constitutes a good parent.

iv Ownership and rights

Surrogacy is characterised by the contract between the intended parents and the surrogate or host mother who will bear the child. The necessity of a contract from the beginning suggests an ambiguity about the ownership, rights and responsibilities to the child.

Mary Beth's contract had stipulated that she should have an amniocentesis. An amniocentesis establishes early in the pregnancy whether the foetus is suffering from any abnormality (Down's Syndrome for instance). Supposing the foetus is considered to be deformed, the question is whether an abortion contrary to the wishes of the surrogate is legally binding. Or in the situation of altruistic surrogacy can the surrogate mother have an abortion (she does not want to give the intended parents a 'damaged' child) contrary to the wishes of the intended parents? There is some ambiguity about who owns the foetus/child. As far as the law is concerned in Britain (see Table 7.1) the surrogate mother is the legal mother until she consents to hand over the baby to the intended parents.

The question of whether the child has a right to know who the surrogate mother is, will be discussed in more detail below when we consider the problem of donors. If it were possible to adopt the coolly rational liberal utilitarian position already referred to, then a surrogate's role is not as a mother but a provider. This is the kind of language used by the charity COTS (Childlessness Overcome Through Surrogacy):

> Using the IVF technique the couple's genetic embryos can be transferred into the surrogate. So basically the surrogate is only acting as an incubator to the genetic child of the couple…The couple can, on a private basis, make an agreement where the surrogate is paid for her expenses and for looking after the child whilst in her womb.

COTS Executive Committee, 1997
quoted in C Donnellan *Surrogacy and IVF* p4

This would suggest that by contract she has no more rights over the child or the child any rights over her than in the exchange of any other goods. Law and contract define ownership. But the utilitarian cannot easily predict long-term consequences. There is no guarantee that when at 18 a child has access to the birth certificate (see Table 7.1) they may not wish to make contact with their 'mother' again.

● Many Christians consider surrogacy (both commercial and altruistic) to violate the view that life cannot be owned by anyone. The principles of the sanctity of life suggest that life is a gift from God (Genesis 1:27, Job 1:21) and that humans do not own it but rather act as its stewards and nurture it. In the Old Testament (Genesis 16:1–12), when Abraham finds that Sarah is barren he takes Hagar, one of his serving girls, and makes her his concubine. Their child is Ishmael. But the story does not condone surrogacy. When eventually Sarah does have a child (Isaac), one of her first acts is to banish Hagar and Ishmael from their home. Ishmael loses his rights of inheritance. Her jealousy and Abraham's feebleness capture the psychological problems associated with surrogacy.

● Although the writer does not condemn surrogacy as such, it is clear that it falls a long way from the ideal (see also Genesis 30 for a similar situation). For the Christian theologian as well as the feminist, the concept of ownership in the case of surrogacy strips Hagar of her basic rights. As soon as she becomes a concubine she even loses the rights of a slave and she and Ishmael are treated not as people but as goods to be disposed of.

v Exploitation and commercial surrogacy

In the 'Baby M' case many argued that Mary Beth's rights as a mother were violated because of her poverty. She had been forced into selling her baby because of wider social conditions which had prevented her from exercising her rights. Commercial surrogacy has therefore been resisted by many countries not only because it is a form of slavery (by selling the child) but a trap for the poor and a loophole for the unscrupulous. (It might make good commercial sense for a surrogacy agency to look for mothers in the Third World where extreme poverty would mean paying the surrogate far less than in the West.) Some philosophers have argued that even had Mary Beth been paid more she would still have been exploited, the money would have become an even more coercive incentive to give up her maternal rights. It was for this reason that some feminists at the time regarded Mary Beth's case as a form of 'commercial prostitution' and a further denigration of women.

Many find the commercialisation of pregnancy deeply repugnant. It reduces human relationships to the market place and turns the baby into a commodity and the mother into a service industry. It also offends Kant's practical imperative never to treat people as a means to an end but an end in themselves.

But there are many who resist these arguments. Commercialisation, they argue, is a part of life and the way that many of our relationships are carried out. The job of the lawyer is to make sure that contracts avoid the confusions of the Baby M case. Furthermore, the contract is a means of distancing the parties from each other and the fee paid avoids unnecessary feelings of obligation from the intended parents to the surrogate. Polly Toynbee argues that surrogacy is no more morally offensive than when a person sells their organs for profit:

1   Some women turn to prostitution, a few to womb-renting. And why not since we have nothing else to offer them?

    By the same token, I see no valid moral argument why the poor should not sell their kidneys if they choose. Most healthy people can
5   function perfectly well with one. The chance to earn a windfall of, say, £50,000, could make a real difference to their lives, and would seem a perfectly rational choice to make.

    In fact a kidney sale is a far better proposition than surrogacy, since the donors are unlikely to mourn their loss the way a mother may
10 mourn her missing child.

P Toynbee *The Independent*, February 1996,
quoted in Donnellan *Surrogacy and IVF* (1997) p12

When Toynbee stated that 'we have nothing else to offer' it admits a failure of society to provide for the poor which necessitates drastic action. It is dubious whether organ selling or womb leasing can ever be an entirely rational act. Mary Beth's lawyer, Harold Cassidy, said after the end of her trial that surrogate mothers 'cannot know, until after the child is born, their true feelings about bearing that child' (quoted in Pence p141).

3 Contraception

> **KEY ISSUE**
>
> ● Does the use of contraception make human sexual relationships more or less loving and responsible?

The use of contraception, whether artificial or natural, means that a couple can have sexual intercourse without the woman becoming pregnant and having a child. The contraceptive pill has not only revolutionised the way in which women have been able to govern their own fertility but given them the sexual freedom to conduct their relationships and their working habits on a par with men.

It is probably more obvious why methods of abortion should be morally controversial as a form of contraception, less clear is why contraception could possibly be wrong if first it maximises freedom of choice and reduces suffering from an unwanted pregnancy.

Some so-called forms of contraceptives work by causing the fertilised egg either to be expelled from the womb or by preventing it from implanting in the womb. Although they are often referred to as contraception, technically they are forms of abortion and better referred to as **abortifacients**.

Even so, although there are clearer reasons why abortifacients might be morally unacceptable there are several important arguments raised by some Christian and secular traditions who consider the use of all forms of artificial contraception as an infringement of human dignity.

a) Theological issues

The major Christian denomination which has consistently argued against the use of artificial contraception has been the Roman Catholic Church. It rejects all forms of artificial contraceptives (even though there are moments when the woman is naturally infertile). This position was famously set out in the Pope's letter *Humanae Vitae* (1968).

I   God has wisely disposed natural laws and rhythms of fecundity which, of themselves, cause a separation in the succession of births. Nonetheless the Church, calling men back to the observance of the norms of the natural law, as interpreted by their constant doctrine,
5   teaches that each and every marriage act must remain open to the transmission of life.

Humanae Vitae

i Unitive and procreative

Humanae Vitae argues that all forms of artificial contraception are wrong (illicit) because they are against natural law: every sexual act (the 'unitive') must intend to result in a child (the 'procreative'). The only exception to this in Roman Catholic teaching is the **rhythm method** when a woman has a safe period (just before ovulation) where nature provides a moment (or 'rhythm' in nature) when a couple can have sexual intercourse without the probability of having a child.

Having a child reminds us that in Catholic theology sex must always be considered in the context of the purpose or 'goods' of marriage. If marriage is a natural state which celebrates the creation, where God instructs man to be 'fruitful and multiply' (Genesis 1:28) then it follows both from the point of Scripture and natural law that contraception frustrates the primary purpose (or *telos*) of a couple to become parents and rear children.

ii Weakness of the natural law position

For many Roman Catholics, however, *Humanae Vitae* has proved to be a disappointment and a lost opportunity for the Church to use its influence to argue for the moral and responsible use of modern reproductive technologies. As we shall see below, its view on the unitive/procreative directly affects its views on other forms of reproduction. The issue has become one of conscience for many Catholics who use contraception based on what they regard as a flawed argument. If the rhythm method is permitted as an exception when nature provides its own contraception then it has to be questioned whether the unitive/procreative ends of sex can be entirely right in all circumstances. If sex does not intend to be procreative every time then artificial contraception should be permitted.

For example, the liberal Catholic psychologist Jack Dominion argues that sex has many purposes all of which serve to enhance the husband-wife relationship. He names four: love, procreation, pleasure and relief of tension; 'the single most important is the presence of love, which represents the highest unity of body and person' (*God, Sex and Love* p30). But, sexual love which is not life-giving is reduced to hedonistic self-seeking. So, by considering sex in terms of psychological life-giving Dominion reinterprets *Humanae Vitae* to include what he considers to be an equally valid non-procreative sexual relationship where both husband and wife are still creative as they grow and sustain each other.

> The full potential of sexual intercourse is to be seen as a source of life for two people who are relating over time. It is powerless to operate when it is experienced in transient, unreliable and unpredictable circumstances.
>
> J Dominion and H Montefiore *God, Sex and Love* (1989) p32

iii Protestant and reform churches

Until fairly recently Protestant and reform churches held a view not dissimilar from the Roman Catholic Church. The primary concern was that contraception would encourage irresponsible behaviour and separate sex from its proper place in marriage. However, most reform/Protestant churches today (Church of England, Methodist, Lutheran) hold that there is a distinction between sex for unitive purposes and sex for procreation and these are reflected in the way in which marriage is considered first to be for companionship and secondly for children (see page 80). There are, in addition, good pragmatic reasons for the use of contraception.

- Couples need to be able to provide for families which they can afford financially. Genesis 1:26–30 calls on humans to be good stewards of the world's resources.
- A responsible control of family size contributes to the well-being of society.
- Because the rhythm method necessitates the woman checking when her ovulation has reached its safe period, far too much emphasis is put on the body and sex (it reduces spontaneity and ritualises sex).

Contraception, therefore, is not necessarily contrary to marriage, but used responsibly is an aid to a loving, intimate relationship between husband and wife.

iv Moral objections to contraception

However, there are other objections to the use of contraception (besides the natural law argument) many of which are shared by those outside the Christian tradition.

- **Respect for persons**. Many feminists have argued that contraception has reinforced male control over women. Most forms of contraception have relied on women regulating their fertility, a practice reinforced by men. How many men would choose sterilisation (vasectomy) or would take an equivalent of 'the pill'? Contraception reduces the companionship element in a relationship by making sex an end itself without consequences. It can diminish male respect for women when they think that sexual intercourse is all that a relationship is about.
- **Means of power**. Some see the opportunities that contraception gives to institutions to interfere with a basic right of every human being to reproduce. For example, since 1983 the Chinese government issued a directive which stated that 'Women with one child have IUDs inserted, one spouse of couples with two or more children be sterilised, and all unauthorised pregnancies be aborted...' . (cited in D Alton Life After Death p80) In that year 21 million sterilisations, 18 million IUD insertions and 14 million abortions took place. And in the West there have been a number of cases where the local health services have enforced contraception or sterilisation on a woman when they have

considered it to be in her 'best interests' (i.e. because she is mentally retarded or dangerous).

● **Exploitation**. Sometimes the Catholic Church has been blamed for causing poorer countries hardship through population explosion by banning contraception. A response to this is often that the size of family is part of much more complex structures. In some cases a small family is simply unable to have the working power to survive. Smaller families destroy the networking which large and extended families enjoy. Poverty is to do with other resources apart from the size of family.

● **Sin**: Some theologians have considered that contraception encourages people to break two of the seven deadly sins. It leads to a lazy morality or sloth, where a relationship requires active self-control and concern for each other. The Protestant theologian Paul Ramsey has argued that contraception is another example of human pride and is the desire to rule over nature and dominate as if we are God (what is termed 'hubris') rather than working with nature. The Pope's letter *Humanae Vitae* added that rejection of the natural order encourages the young to discard other aspects of the natural – it can lead to fornication (sex without marriage) and adultery (sex outside marriage). The lack of serious consequences (i.e. through the birth of a child) has legitimised sexual permissiveness and harmed the institution of marriage and the family.

b) Sterilisation and celibacy

Is it permissible for a couple to marry and abstain from having children? Or having had children either to be sterilised or to refrain from sexual intercourse? The options are very different. In refraining from sexual intercourse both man and woman by mutual consent opt for celibacy, whereas sterilisation does not. But a more important distinction is that celibacy is only temporary whereas sterilisation removes all possibility for having children. From a Roman Catholic perspective although occasional celibacy may serve an important role in marriage, sterilisation deliberately frustrates the purpose of marriage and is a mortal sin.

i St Paul

> Do not refuse one another except perhaps by agreement for a season, that you may devote yourselves to prayer; but then come together again, lest Satan tempt you through lack of self-control.

1 Corinthians 7:5

Whereas St Paul makes it quite clear that celibacy for the single person rules out all sexual relationships, he argues within the Jewish tradition that sex between husband and wife is to be enjoyed equally and mutually. Without sexual intercourse a marriage would cease to be a proper marriage. The exception here is envisaged for a short period of time and then only for religious reasons such as prayer and fasting. It is important to note that Paul does not think that sex is in anyway defiling or that it invalidates the religious life.

ii St Augustine

St Augustine's argument begins with Paul's statement, 'I wish that all were as I myself am' (1 Corinthians 7:6) – that is single, celibate and chaste (sexually pure). On the one hand, Augustine argued that sex is not in itself sinful – indeed sex was always possible even in the perfect state within the Garden of Eden, nevertheless the desire for sex illustrates the presence of men and women's fallen state (see page 12). Augustine was impressed by those married couples who were also able to abstain from sexual relationships and live the 'continent' or the life most resistant to sin, but he realised also that the sex-drive is too strong simply to be replaced by celibacy.

iii Catholic Church

The *Catechism of the Catholic Church* permits the periodic use of voluntary celibacy so that couples can plan or regulate births of children. But, 'It is their duty to make certain that their desire is not motivated by selfishness but is in conformity with the generosity appropriate to responsible parenthood' (*Catechism* p507). In other words, St Paul's teaching (1 Corinthians 7:5) may be applied through mutual loving abstinence. But as Augustine said, the sex drive may not so easily be controlled. Even in a loving relationship it may be much harder for a woman to deny her husband his conjugal rights even though she may not want to increase the size of her family. In other words, abstinence is simply unrealistic and can put undue emotional strain on a modern marriage.

c) Abortifacients

So far the arguments above have assumed that the forms of contraception being discussed have worked by hindering fertilisation. But there are a number of 'contraceptive' means – chemical and mechanical – which should more accurately be called **abortifacients**. Abortifacts work by causing the body to reject the fertilised egg or embryo. Finally, abortion itself may be used as a form of birth control. Under discussion in this context are the 'coil' or **IUD** (intra-uterine device), the **morning after pill** and the 'abortion pill' **RU486**.

The argument here hinges on the issue as to whether and at what stage the embryo/foetus can be considered a person. The arguments are complex (see Michael Wilcockson *Issues of Life and Death* Chapter 3) but the use of these forms of birth control depends on:

- whether a foetus is a person from the moment of conception.
- whether the foetus becomes a person at a defined later stage.

i Conception

Both the coil and morning after pill work either by inhibiting conception or by causing the body to reject the fertilised egg or zygote from implanting in the womb. It is hard to say at what stage fertilisation takes place and therefore whether the method used is a contraception or an abortion. Unlike other methods there is strong possibility that IUD and morning after pill are forms of abortion.

For many both these methods are no more morally excusable than surgical forms of abortion. The moment of conception brings a new human life into being which, all being well, will develop into a fully grown person.

> Human life must be respected and protected absolutely from the moment of conception. From the first moment of his existence a human being must be recognised as having the rights of a person – among which is the inviolable right of every innocent being to life.
>
> *Catechism of the Catholic Church* (1994) page 489

Sometimes the justification for these methods is that they merely cause the body to miscarry which it does naturally: only 20 out of 100 conceptions will survive to be born. But pro-life organisations such as SPUC, LIFE as well as the Catholic Church argue that this is false reasoning. A miscarriage is when the body spontaneously causes the womb to reject the embryo/foetus. This is quite different from the intentional termination of an innocent life. Yet under the Human Fertilisation and Embryology Act (1990), the coil and morning after pill are considered contraceptives and not abortifacients.

ii Pre-embryo

However, not every one is persuaded that individual human life comes into being at conception. The Human Fertilisation and Embryology Act, for instance, selected another important moment for foetal development. Around 14 days the 'primitive streak' becomes apparent. (This is when the cells divide and begin to form the first distinct layers and cells of the inner cell mass. After the 14th day the rudiments of the primary cell and nervous system appear.) Before that time it is possible for the cells to split and form monozygotic twins, so it is only at this moment that we can talk about an individual life. If this is the case then there is some justification for considering IUD and the morning after pill as contraceptives and not abortifacients, if by abortion we mean the termination of an actual human life.

iii Brain activity

Finally, some argue that the foetus can only be regarded as a person once there is continuous brain activity. The attractiveness of this view is that the principle can also be used to determine whether to end a

life of a person with severe brain damage and in persistent vegetative
states. Spasmodic brain activity usually occurs around 54 days. This is
within the recommended threshold for the use of RU486 (often given
to be 49 days after a missed period).

In 1991, the British Department of Health granted a licence for the
use of 'Mifepristone' or 'Mifegyne'. Although its use is covered by the
Abortion Act (1967), it may also be administered by doctors in their
surgeries and family planning clinics – and not just in hospitals and
clinics in the usual way for an abortion.

iv Side-effects

There is still quite a considerable debate as to how safe and effective
some of these forms of contraceptive are. All forms of chemical
contraceptives pose some risk. The contraceptive pill can cause breast
cancer and thrombosis. Far more problematic is RU486. Although it
offers a far less gruesome form of abortion (3 tablets are taken orally
to block the hormone progesterone which is essential to maintain the
pregnancy, another causes the foetus to be expelled), some 4% of
cases fail to expel the entire foetus and there is often the risk of heavy
bleeding and infection. There is some evidence that it loses its
effectiveness with repeated use.

The morning after pill or emergency contraceptive has a 75%
effectiveness. Some of its side-effects are nausea and headaches. The
use of the IUD can cause infertility.

4 *In vitro* fertilisation and assisted reproduction

KEY ISSUE

● What limits, if any, should be put on human reproductive
technologies?

We began this chapter by looking at surrogacy as an example of the
powerful emotional and psychological forces which characterise the
human desire to reproduce. Other chapters on marriage and the
family also illustrate the wish to have children is a crucial contribution
to the relationship between men and women and perhaps also in gay
and lesbian unions as well. The debate over contraception adds two
other important considerations; firstly whether every sexual act
should be open to procreation, and secondly what it means to be a
responsible parent.

Reproductive technology is not just about enabling childless
couples to form families as close to the natural process itself, but also
to bring children into the world who will have the best possible
conditions in which to flourish. Technology has not only enabled

'infertile' couples to conceive, but in addition provides the means for filtering out genetic defects through gene therapy and human cloning. Some feel this goes too far. Whereas many feel that reproductive technologies are good if they can help nature along the way, they draw the line at any further intrusion.

Advances in technologies change daily and so do the range and complexity of moral issues.

a) Infertility, marriage and patriarchy

i Infertility
Infertility is a broad term. Anthony Dyson (*The Ethics of IVF* 1995 p11) outlines the four stages of the reproduction process where a pregnancy may fail:

● failure to find adequate sperm or eggs
● failure to conceive (egg and sperm do not meet)
● the fertilised gamete fails to implant into the lining of the uterus
● repeated failure of early pregnancies.

Between 10-15% of couples are infertile in the West. More precisely this means that whereas 90% of couples may conceive in the first year and 96% in the second year of trying for a child, around 45% of women lose their pregnancy without knowing and some 15% miscarry. Women account for some 50 to 70% of all infertility, men between 20 to 30% of all infertility.

ii Marriage
For many in the Christian tradition one of the primary 'goods' or purposes of marriage is to have children. Infertility, for whatever reason, is the cause of considerable anguish as this husband recounts:

1 If I cannot give my wife the baby she wants, I do not have anything worthy of giving to anyone I love... My wife and I have come to a resolution of our infertility as a couple. We are the adoptive parents of a fine girl who thrives and finds our love... I accept my infertility, but I
5 will never, fully, be reconciled to it.

quoted in A Dyson *The Ethics of IVF* (1995) p13

To this end assisted reproduction helps complete a marriage and form a family.

iii Children are not a right but a gift
Despite the benefits of assisted reproduction, there are many who argue that these technologies have wrongly suggested that every couple has a right to a child. This is mostly clearly stated by the Roman Catholic Church which also, it will be remembered, argued

that sex within marriage is primarily for the procreation of children. The reasons given are that children are a gift (e.g. Genesis 4:1, Psalm 127:3) not a right of parents and in addition any process which interrupts the unitive and procreative purpose of sex is illicit. A sterile couple may channel their energies into other creative acts such as 'adoption, various forms of educational work and assistance to other families and to the poor or handicapped children' (*On Respect for Life*).

Is infertility better considered as a health issue rather than a 'natural' state of affairs? If so should it be treated through public health care?

● Infertility is an illness or disease like many others which may afflict otherwise healthy people. It can therefore be treated.
● If infertility is considered a malfunction or aberration of nature, then the use of technology may help rectify the fault and put the process back on its natural course.

iv Technology and patriarchy

We saw in the case of Baby M (see pages 128–133) that for many naturalist or radical feminists (see Chapter 3 pages 28–29), certain forms of reproductive technologies represent an unacceptable level of intrusion into a woman's life. IVF in particular necessitates a long series of hormone treatment, extraction of eggs, and surgical operations. It is physically and emotionally draining and expensive. But the chief objection is that it removes the control a woman has over her own body; technology is a form of patriarchy exercising its power over her body manipulating it to reproduce. For some, thinking in Marxist terms, it is an example of an oppressive society where the means of production or rather reproduction have been obliquely removed from women. By using technology controlled by men it has allowed an external power to interfere and manipulate at every stage. So whereas some feminists have seen the technological revolution as the great liberation (DI for instance can liberate her from the demands of a genetic father, or in some cases for a male relationship altogether) others have been far more hesitant.

In her novel *The Handmaid's Tale* (Vintage 1985), the feminist novelist Margaret Atwood invents a future dystopia where reproductive technology has turned tail reducing women to their various sexual functions. There are Marthas who clean and cook; Jezebels or prostitutes who provide sexual pleasure; Handmaids or reproductive prostitutes; Wives or infertile women who act as social secretaries. The whole system is geared so that men can engineer the right conditions to have perfect offspring divorced from love and affection. Children and women have become no more than commodities and producers. Atwood's message clearly warns women against the unthinking use of technology which can unwittingly become another form of patriarchy and exploitation of women.

b) Reproductive technologies

Reproductive technologies serve three purposes. Firstly to help male infertility (AIH and DI), secondly to aid female infertility (IVF, GIFT, ED and OD) and thirdly to screen against genetic abnormalities. Table 7.2 below sets out the chief methods and some of the ethical issues each raises. (For a more detailed account of each process see for example Anthony Dyson *The Ethics of IVF.*)

c) Identity and parents

Should it make any difference whether a child's parents are genetically related to him or her? There are two issues here.

● Does the use of a donor (through any of DI, ED or OD) in any way adversely affect the child's own sense of identity in later life?
● Will either of the social parents feel any less about their child if it is not genetically related to them?

There is no empirical way of knowing the answers to either of these questions although experience of adopting children has provided some insight.

i Analogy with adoption

The Church of England's revised report *Personal Origins* (1996) argues that the most important issue at stake is *openness* and honesty. Providing a child knows how and why they have been brought into being then the question of exact genetic origin is of little concern. In other words, if a child can understand the *story* of their own identity in terms of a willed and loving action this is the essential ingredient for their own sense of self-worth.

The report is aware that being open and honest is not without its problems. In order for the child to feel secure then grandparents, friends and existing children, not just parents, have to accept that the child is needed and loved. By the same token a great deal of psychological damage can be done when a child is told that he or she was a 'mistake' and that conception was unintentional.

Nevertheless, just as in adoption children often do want to know about their origins. However, the analogy with adoption is not entirely the same. Whereas in the case of adoption there is a birth mother with her own history and reasons for giving away a child, a donor did not create or give away a life. Even so it might be argued that the insistence that egg or sperm should not be sold but given freely as an act of generosity acknowledges that the provision of genetic material is more than inert substance. It is understandable therefore why some children should want to know why they are the way they are and in order for their own story to be complete they need more than a genetic or biological account of their donor. Some argue that

Table 7.2 Summary of some forms of assisted reproduction

Method	Process	Reasons and Risks	Issues
AIH Artificial Donation by Husband (or partner)	The husband or partner's sperm is introduced into the woman's vagina using a syringe.	Helps where a man is unable to get an erection, is disabled, has a low sperm count or is suffering from a sexually transmitted disease. There are no physical side-effects.	The process has been used for at least 50 years. One major objection is that it separates unitive sex (loving process) from the procreative (the reproductive). Another is whether all forms of AIH turn the child into a commodity rather than a gift.
DI Donor Insemination by donor (formerly called AID – artificial insemination by donor).	Same as AIH except that sperm is given by an anonymous donor.	Helps where a man's sperm are defective or would transfer an hereditary genetic disease. The HFE Act limits the number of children to 10 per donor. The social father is considered to be the legal father unless he fails to consent. Since 1996 no fee is paid to the donor.	Problems of identity. Who will the child regard as his or her 'real' father? Clash of rights between the child's right to know v. anonymity of the donor. Is the introduction of a 'third' party equivalent to adultery or another form of adoption? Could the donor be a genetic relative (the husband's brother for instance)? Is it right for a lesbian couple to use DI?
IVF *In vitro* fertilisation	The woman's egg and partner's sperm are fertilised outside the womb 'in glass' (i.e. *in vitro*) or a petri dish and then at the two to eight cell stage transferred to the uterus. The woman is given progesterone so that the lining of the womb is ready for implantation.	Helps where a woman's fallopian tubes are blocked or damaged, or when she produces anti-bodies which react to her partner's semen and kill his sperm. The process allows for genetic screening for disorders and the possibility for 'engineering' where defects are found. Very painful side effects of drugs to produce eggs for 'harvesting' which requires surgical operation for extraction. Psychologically draining; the woman feels that her body is not her own because it is subject to many tests. It is expensive (e.g. £2460 per treatment at the Oxford Fertility Unit, 1998). There is a high chance of failure (12.5% successful live births in 1990). There is an increased chance of multiple births.	The present process produces more fertilised gametes than are needed. HFE Act permits up to three to be placed in the womb. Having initiated a pregnancy is it morally right to 'reduce' the number of foetuses later (i.e. abortion). The HFE Act was amended in 1996 to allow freezing of frozen eggs for up to 10 years. What is their status? Can they be destroyed they are if not needed? The Act allows experiments to be carried out up to 14 days on fertilised eggs. Is this right? Is gene therapy, which allows for the modification of defective cells, interfering too much with nature or a responsible form of parenting?

Method	Process	Reasons and Risks	Issues
GIFT Gamete Intra-Fallopian Transfer	Egg and sperm are collected in the same way as IVF except the fertilised egg(s) is placed in the fallopian tube(s).	The woman produces too much cervical mucus which prohibits the sperm reaching the fallopian tubes. High risk of ectopic pregnancies – which can endanger the mother's life.	Not governed by the HFEA because fertilisation takes place in the fallopian tubes (not *in vitro*) and continues as a normal pregnancy.
ED Embryo donation	Uses the same process as IVF but uses donor egg and sperm.	Where neither the man or woman are able to produce sperm or egg ED may be used. The social mother can bond more fully with the foetus. Donations are often given as a result of IVF for other infertile couples where extra embryos have been created.	Resolves the problems of what to do with extra and unwanted fertilised eggs, but now creates another donor parent. A child therefore will have two genetic parents and two social parents. Does the intimacy of bonding and birth outweigh the possible problems of identity?
OD Ovum donation	Uses the same process as IVF but uses a donor egg.	See DI. Since 1996 no fee may be paid to the donor.	The same problems as DI, except that demand for donors far outstrips supply. Should eggs be used from aborted foetuses?
Cloning	Nucleus substitution: the nucleus is removed from a fertilised egg and replaced with the nucleus from an adult human cell. Embryonic biopsy: Genetically identical individuals are created through division of the embryo at a very early stage.	Enables genetic tests to be carried out on the early foetus. If the tests prove that the foetus is free from defect then the cloned foetus can be placed back in the womb. Creates 'spare parts' which are genetically compatible for when a person falls ill later in life. But success rates are low and in the case of nucleus substitution no one knows what the long term effects will be.	Morally this is the most intrusive of all reproductive processes. What will the long-term effects be? Will it create a form of human underclass to be used purely for their bodily spare parts? Is it necessary at all? What are the alternatives?

HFE Act = *The Human Fertilisation and Embryology Act (1990)*
HFEA = *The Human Fertilisation and Embryology Authority (authorised to oversee the provisions of the Act)*

although legally a child may, at present, have access to information about their donor's characteristics, it will only be a matter of time before children will have a right to know who their genetic parent actually is. Inevitably this might lead to complicated emotional problems: an intrusion of the donor's child later into his life, where he or she may have their own family), could very well cause all kinds of emotional problems.

ii Analogy with adultery

The use of 'adultery' here is being used to suggest that the use of donors confuses proper family relationships. The analogy with adultery cannot be used in its ordinary sense, for whereas adultery involves a relationship outside marriage or committed cohabitation, the introduction of a donor does not involve any direct sexual relationship.

But critics of the use of donors argue that a social parent could well feel that the introduction of a 'third party' into the relationship alienates them from their children. Parents might feel that whenever a child behaves in a way that is critical of them that this is due to their different genetic origins and that the child is fundamentally not their own, however much they love him or her.

The issue is particularly acute when the donor is a member of the close family. In order to overcome some of the identity problems which a child might feel using an anonymous donor, then it would be better to use a donor genetically very close to the social parent. A daughter might donate an egg (OD) to her mother, or a sister to a sister, or a mother to her son's wife. If the parents are to heed the openness suggested by *Personal Origins* then how will a child relate to the person whom he knows as his aunt but is in fact also his genetic mother? The emotional problems are similar to the ones which we observed in the case of surrogacy. This explains why many, such as the report *Personal Origins* does, reject known donors (as well as surrogacy) in preference for anonymous donors.

iii Posthumous fertilisation

Another related set of problems relates to the problem of parental consent and the child's identity after a spouse has died. In most cases it is assumed that by having sperm, egg or embryo fertilised then by intention consent has been implied for it to be used later. In the case of **Diane Blood** (1998) the HFEA had originally refused her permission to use her dead husband's sperm because he had not given written consent. Mrs Blood had taken and frozen her husband's sperm whilst he lay in a coma after he contracted bacterial meningitis in 1995. The question is whether marriage constitutes *implicit* consent given that the purpose, especially in Christian marriage, is for the procreation of children. In the end the Court of Appeal judged that in this case, though consent was not explicitly given, it could not stop her using AI outside the UK.

But is it right deliberately to bring a child into the world either in old age, or without a partner, and without explicit consent? Most theological responses consider that marriage requires both partners to be present and give explicit consent to have a child. If this is not the case the onus on the utilitarian is to show that there are no long-term harmful consequences to parent or child.

If explicit consent is not always necessary then is there anything morally objectionable about using an aborted foetus' eggs? Table 7.2 poses the moral problem. If eggs are in short supply and a female foetus has 400,000 to 2 million eggs in her ovaries, might it not be argued that rather than waste this resource it should be used to help many others?

- **Consent**: An essential element of the liberal principle is that consent should be given. A foetus is unable to do so. However, this is irrelevant if in the case of abortion consent is already acknowledged to lie with the mother who has agreed to the abortion.
- **Slippery slope**: If it is accepted that aborted foetuses may be used for egg donation, then what are the moral objections to breeding foetuses for other 'spare parts'? Is the status of the foetus entirely dependent on whether it is or is not wanted? Those who hold a sanctity of life position argue that there is something morally repulsive about disposing of a human life and then plundering it.
- **Identity**: Yet again the issue of identity is challenged. Is it just a question of irrational sentiment or taste which objects to the thought that a child's genetic parent never fully existed or was deliberately destroyed or might a child be educated into being grateful to be alive whatever their origins?

d) Gene therapy and human cloning

i Making human beings

In 1970, 16 years before the birth of the first IVF baby, Louise Brown in 1986, the outspoken Protestant theologian **Paul Ramsey** warned, in his prophetic book *Fabricated Man* (1970), against the development of technology which would fail to treat human life with the dignity that it deserves. He rejected IVF mostly because he considered that it would increase human defects not reduce them. Even though many of the risks he envisaged have not occurred, the principle which Ramsey established cuts across theological and secular thinking.

- As **co-creators** with God we have a duty to create a good world.
- If there is to be a genetic defect in a child then the only ethical form of genetic control must be passive i.e. to refrain from procreation. Theologically the use of sterilisation 'may be morally obligatory'. In fact if Christians have a duty to bring healthy children into the world, then they should also see it as their duty to remain celibate. This is in direct contrast to the Roman Catholic view of marriage.

● **Active genetic** control is not acceptable. Whereas the utilitarian scientist might argue that if the human 'machinery' is defective it should be improved Ramsey considered the purpose of creation is to enable a relationship of love between humans and God. Thus he preferred the term 'procreation' (creating as God does through love) rather than 'reproduction' (mechanical). Although he felt that in general DI and ED severed the loving intentions of procreation, his real objection was against the use of cloning.

● **Cloning** symbolises the domination of technology over ourselves. It destroys human relationships based on love and co-operation. Technology of this kind is a form of divorce which 'puts asunder' what God and humans create through loving sexual relationships. The real risk is that what we create might not be good, but rather a series of appalling blunders which cannot be morally or theologically justifiable.

Ramsey concludes:

> Men ought not to play God before they learn to be men, and after they have learned to be men, they will not play God

> P Ramsey *Fabricated Man* (1970) p138

ii *Experiments on the embryo*

One of the most controversial aspects of the **Warnock Report** (reprinted as *A Question of Life* 1985), which became the foundation of the 1990 Human Fertilisation and Embryology Act, was its recommendation that gene therapy and experimentation on 'pre-embryos' could take place up to 14 days from conception – that is just before the primitive streak appears and the embryo can be considered to have become an individual person.

The justification is essentially a utilitarian one. If experiments on the 'pre-embryo' can further scientific knowledge to help overcome problems of infertility and other genetic problems in the future, then its goods outweigh any other emotional or moral hesitations one might have. It is an argument which works providing one accepts the conclusion that a 14-day-old 'pre-embryo' is not a person.

There are several points to consider here:

● **First order** arguments find it morally reprehensible that human life of any kind should be subject to experimentation.

● **Second order** objections state that as the embryo cannot give its informed consent in line with current medical practice, experimentation is wrong.

● The report itself is considered to be very inconsistent here. First it argues that utilitarianism is not sufficient to deal with these complex issues. Then, in this case, justification is given based on utilitarian principles.

iii Gene therapy

The first consideration in gene therapy is to establish the status of the genetic defect. Traditionally decisions are based on two kinds of therapy (sometimes referred to as 'engineering'):

- **Negative therapy**: that is the *removal* of defects or diseases by selection.
- **Positive therapy**: that is the *improvement* of human qualities by alteration to the genes.

However, how does one decide which condition is a defect and the other an improvement unless there is an already established view of the 'normal' human being. To some extent the distinction is culturally determined and can only be judged vaguely by public reaction. Which of the following would be considered the removal of a defect or an improvement?

> The alteration of the gene which causes cystic fibrosis.
> The alteration of the gene which causes Down's syndrome.
> The alteration of sex genes to select the sex of a child.
> The alteration of the gene (if it exists) which causes homosexuality.

Two considerations must be borne in mind. The first might be an anti-reductionist claim which considers that no single gene can ever adequately determine a major aspect of a person's character. The second is cautious of entering the world of **eugenics** – the deliberate engineering of certain types of human beings based on an ideology of what constitutes the perfect person.

- **Passive control:** Couples can be tested prior to having a child for genetic counselling and encouraging a person not to have a child. Or during pregnancy be encouraged to have an abortion.
- **Active control**: Direct interference either in the form of **somatic gene therapy** whereby the alteration or addition of genes to cells in the body change its characteristics (but not for future generations) or **germ line gene therapy**. This latter process constitutes the alteration or addition of genes in sperm, egg or embryo and will cause all future generations to be so modified.

For many theologians the key notion here is responsibility. The authors of *Personal Origins*, for instance, argue that parents who remove *serious* genetic defects are acting in a far more loving and responsible way than parents who have children and then either divorce or separate. The question of germ-line therapy will depend on what science may reasonably predict and then, after caution and considerable debate, it may be used.

iv Human cloning

What are the reasons for wanting to clone humans? At present there are two main purposes:

- **Reproductive cloning**: A human clone would provide exact matches for blood transfusions, cancer treatment, kidney failure and so on. At a very early stage of foetal development a clone could be tested and diagnosed to see whether the non-cloned embryo was free from abnormality.
- **Therapeutic cloning**: By cloning the 'stem cells' (i.e. cells which have yet to take on any particular function) then the cells can be switched on to produce particular human organs for spare parts. The 'clones' in this case are not human beings but human organs which would be an exact match to the foetus from whom they were taken.

There are two means of creating a clone:

- **Nucleus transfer**: The nucleus is removed from a fertilised egg and replaced with the nucleus from an adult human cell to create a genetic 'carbon copy' embryo of that adult.
- **Embryonic splitting** (or 'biopsy'). Genetically identical individuals are created through division of the embryo's cells before the primitive streak stage (this could occur naturally to create identical twins)

In 1991, Robin Gill wrote commenting on Ramsey's speculations, 'The more fanciful elements – such as human nucleus substitution, trans-species fertilisation involving human genetic material, human partheno-genesis or ectogenesis – remain as fanciful as ever.' (*Christian Ethics in Secular Worlds*, 1991). But at that stage the cloning of Dolly the Sheep (1997) had not taken place and what may have looked like science fiction is rapidly appearing to become science fact. If people worry about the effects of genetically modified foods on our environment and human society, how will future human clones affect the future of human existence?

Some of the major concerns are:

- **Utilitarian risks**. Concerns must take into account the enormous risks involved. There are no guarantees that a clone will live a happy normal life: it may die early, age more quickly or develop unforeseen disabilities.
- **Slippery slope**. Many fear that if therapeutic cloning is permitted (i.e. for spare organ parts), then it will only be a matter of time before reproductive cloning will be allowed.
- **Exploitation and rights**. Is it right to create second class humans to be exploited by others for their spare parts? On what grounds could it be said that a clone does not have the same rights as any other human being? David Alton finds the prospect deeply disturbing and considers the process to be what he calls 'technological cannibalism' (D Alton *Life After Death* p113).
- **Identity and eugenics**. The problem of identity can be seen in two ways. Firstly, how will society consider a clone? Will the clone be a person with an independent identity from its original? Secondly, how will the clone perceive itself? Would it consider itself to have an independent

identity of its own or think of itself as morally and spiritually inferior to its original? If the latter, then it seems to be getting very close to the grossly immoral forms of eugenics practised by Hitler and others who considered some humans to be racially and biologically inferior.

● **Theology of marriage.** Asexual procreation cannot be accepted within any Christian tradition which considers the female/male bond in marriage to mirror the God/world relationship. In other words, the process of creating life is not just a biological one, but one which requires the intimacy and love of two individuals to create another human being who is also loved and wanted. Cloning confuses and destroys this intimate process of procreation.

Answering structured and essay questions

Questions

1. **a)** Explain why certain forms of contraceptives are considered morally less acceptable than others.
    b) 'Surrogacy destroys the natural bond between child and parents and should not be allowed' Discuss.

2. **a)** Explain why Christian theology is divided over whether sex should always be unitive and procreative.
    b) Discuss whether the use of donors in IVF treatment for infertile couples is morally acceptable.

3. To what extent is germ-line human gene therapy a prospect so dangerous and uncertain that it should always be made illegal?

4. 'Every human being has a right to reproduce' Discuss.

5. Assess the view that experiments on human embryos are always wrong.

Essay skills

It is important that essays should not become bogged down by long descriptions of methods and processes to do with infertility and contraception. These are only necessary when there is some specific moral issue at stake (such as the way an IUD works as an abortifacient). The important philosophical ideas which will need careful attention each time are: natural law, utilitarianism, liberty/autonomy, sanctity of life and rights. Make sure terms are defined carefully. 'Surrogacy' refers to several processes; 'natural bond' hints not only at the psychological/spiritual problems but the issue of 'contract'. Many of the arguments, and especially theological ones, depend on being clear what is meant by 'sex' – the unitive/procreative distinction can be used in many contexts.

Summary diagram on reproductive ethics

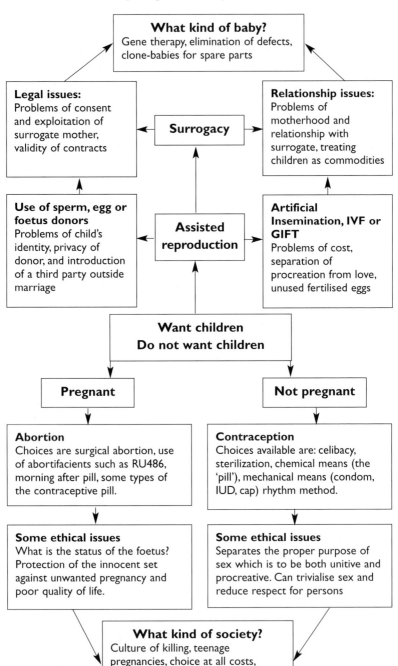

8 Family relationships

KEYWORDS

affinity – a family relationship established through legal or spiritual recognition

child abuse – the exercise of sexual power over a child by a parent or carer for self-gratification

Children Act, 1989 – an important piece of legislation in England and Wales which reflects many of the changes taking place in the family

conjugal bond – the married state of a man and woman

consanguinity – all those who share the same 'blood', a blood relation

dowry – money or property traditionally given by a woman's father on her marriage (also known as bride price)

extended family – the wider set of family relations (legal and blood) who may or may not live in close proximity

household rules – the rules of family duties developed by Roman and Greeks and incorporated by early Christian writers

incest – an illicit sexual relationship between people regarded too close to marry (as determined through familiar affinity and consanguinity)

kinship – relationship established through consanguinity and/or affinity.

nuclear family – man and woman and children living in their own accommodation and being self contained

paterfamilias – (Latin) a family or household presided over by a senior man

1 Is the family in crisis?

KEY ISSUE

● Has there ever been a time when the ideal family existed?

Is the family in crisis? Consider the picture on page 154 and the words of the marriage service (from the Anglican Alternative Service Book,

1980) below it. The status of the family is driven by political, ideological and religious expectations. The picture assumes a 'golden period' of the family in the post-war period: a mother who stays at home to look after the children and a father who works to support his loving family. The Christian ideal confirms that the family is an extension of heterosexual marriage: companionate, life-long and the place where children are reared in a loving stable environment. Whatever may be concluded about the present state of the family, the constitution of the family is seen to have direct bearing on society as a whole. If the family really is in crisis then it might suggest that in some way that society is also morally and politically in turmoil.

THE TRADITIONAL NUCLEAR FAMILY

Christian marriage

- "Marriage is given, that husband and wife may comfort and help each other..."
- "It is given... that they may know each other in love..."
- "It is given, that they may have children and be blessed in caring for them and bringing them up in accordance with God's will, to his praise and glory."
- "In marriage husband and wife belong to one another, and they begin a new life together in the community."
- Both husband and wife make public promises that they will look after each other "for better, for worse; for richer for poorer; in sickness and in health; to love and to cherish; till death us do part"
- The priest concludes by quoting from Jesus' words "That which God has joined together, let not man divide"

Recently, *The Times* reported the Brisish Home Secretary, Jack Straw, as having said, 'There never was a golden period of the family' (5 November 1998). The remark suggests something of the dilemma which the family poses for any government passing legislation, or for a school educating its children into socially accepted norms or parents themselves in the passing on of values. On one level Straw's remark states the obvious. There have always been unhappy families; there have always been those who have suffered under oppressive fathers, negligent mothers and cramped living conditions. On another much more significant level, Straw's comment suggests that the notion of a single, universal family ideal has never existed. The picture above was never universally true because the notion of the nuclear family is essentially a middle-class, bourgeois, Western (Northern European/North American) product of the mid 20th century during a time of industrial prosperity. And the Christian family ideal expressed in this particular marriage service book (1980) is typical of current theological thought but subtly different from the Anglican Prayer Book of 1662 where the primary aim of marriage was for regularising sex and the procreation of children (see page 80).

Ronald Fletcher (*The Shaking of the Foundations* 1988, pp17–20) suggests that there are three responses to the suggestion that the family is in crisis:

- The family is undergoing a major period of decline.
- The family is not in decline, but possibly too powerful.
- The family is simply going through a period of change.

a) The family in decline

This view argues that the traditional family structure has been eroded socially and morally because of the following:

- Ease of **divorce**. 40% of British marriages end in divorce; 55% involve children under 16. Increase in step-parents and psychological damage to children.
- Increasing independence of **women** (sexually and financially).
- **Artificial insemination**, surrogacy and the ability to have donor children have changed attitudes to children and what constitutes kinship.
- Increasing numbers of single or **lone parents**. Births outside marriage rose from 64,200 to 222,900 (1940–1995), with an increasing number of teenage pregnancies.
- Decline in **religious weddings**. 58% of marriages in1998 were civil ceremonies.
- Openness to **homosexuality** and challenges to traditional relationships.
- Social acceptability of the less stable state of **cohabitation**. In 1995, there were 268,300 marriages in the UK (the lowest since 1966) and 147,500 divorces.
- Freer attitudes to casual **sexual** relationships.

b) The family is too powerful

The opposite view considers that the crisis of the family has been to alienate many in society by imposing a norm which is incompatible with the desired life-style of what ordinary people want. So, present conditions have not eroded the family but on the contrary made the family unacceptably traditional, inward looking and anti-social. Fletcher argues that the latter part of the 20th century has not diminished the function of the family but rather increased it through social welfare and benefits, insurance, pensions, etc. The Church of England report *The Family in Contemporary Society* (1958) concluded, 'the modern family is in some ways in a stronger position that it has been at any period in our history of which we have knowledge.' But, as Fletcher notes, those who argue for the abolition of the family were not arguing against the family as such but rather for drastic reforms of society which would require a radically different model of the family. Some radicals, such as David Cooper (*The Death of the Family*, 1980) have suggested the Western European family is the cause of many social problems:

- **Intensity** causes mental stress and illness, conflict, sexual repression, violent rebellion.
- **Affluence** of society as a whole has increased the desire of poorer families to want to have what the media presents which increases crime and dissatisfaction and disfunctioning of the family.
- **Privatisation** of the family causes greater discrepancy between rich and poor and furthers class tension in society.

c) The family in a period of change

The third view acknowledges that increase in wealth and material living conditions of Western families since the Second World War and of many new liberties and freedoms have indeed improved the lives of a huge number of people. Divorce has allowed people to develop more flexible and harmonious lives taking into account our greater life expectancy and merely acknowledges that in the past people either lived unhappy lives or found ways round the social restrictions. But at the same time these freedoms have also caused unhappiness and irresponsible behaviour. The third view, argues Fletcher, is 'one of perplexity' because it is unclear whether the undoubted gains are not also accompanied by some blatant losses: have children gained or missed out on freer adult relationships? Have adults themselves faired better or worse with more flexible working conditions and a wider range of permitted relationships?

2 Family and society

> **KEY ISSUE**
> ● How is a family to be defined? Legally, psychologically or biologically?

There is then a widely held view that the Western family is undergoing quite significant changes which are having a direct effect on society as a whole. Implicit in the moral decline view is that in the past the family was stronger and a more significant building block in the fabric of society. An important element of the abolitionist view is that the nuclear family in particular is the product of the modern capitalist industrial society. Jack Straw's remark that there never was a golden period of the family presumes that there is an ideal family and an ideal society which has not hitherto existed. It would be impossible ever to judge whether any period in history has ever satisfied the social ideal, yet so much of this debate assumes that at least at some stage the ideal family actually existed.

It is indicative of the moral, political and social importance of this question that a great deal has been done among social historians to correct, enlarge and revise our knowledge of the family as it existed in the past. This knowledge is enormously important. Firstly, it ensures that value judgements about the present state of the family are properly made. Secondly, history reminds us that what was promoted as the ideal (through church and state) was often very different in reality.

a) Myths about the Western European family

The moral and political debate about the state of the family has been greatly influenced by the research of social historians; **Lawrence Stone** (*The Family, Sex and Marriage in England 1500–1800*, 1977) has been particularly influential. The comprehensive survey by Burguiere, Klapisch-Zuber, Segalen and Zonabend in *A History of the Family* (1996), makes the following revisions of some commonly held misconceptions about the Western European family in the modern period (1500–present day):

● **Uniformity:** The notion of a traditional family is difficult to pin down. Different types of families have developed according to geographical location, economic conditions and prevailing social ideologies. The nuclear family for instance is not a modern phenomenon (as some such as Stone argue), although the restricted nuclear family has become increasingly the norm in post-industrial Western Europe. One characteristic prevails: families of whatever kind are conservative and resist change.

- **Size**: Not all families in the past were large. Couples often married late. The size of the family depended either on the need to supply a cheap workforce or as a sign of power. But in many cases a large family was a major drain on family resources (this was particularly so when the marriage of a girl required a dowry); the average size of household in England 1576–1821 was 4.7 persons. There is evidence that families at all levels of society practised some form of contraception to regulate the size of their families.
- **Stability**: Pre-1750 one in four marriages were re-marriages due to the death of wife or husband. 'The chief feature of the traditional European family was its instability' (*A History of the Family* p15). Plague (e.g. 1600–1670), war (e.g. the 30 Years' War, 1618–48) and weather (e.g. 1580–1600, the 'little ice age') were all responsible for increased likelihood of children being brought up by step-parents or other family members.
- **Love and consent**: In many cases marriages were used as the only means by which a family could ensure an income, as we can observe in the use of the pre-marriage contract in the 18th century to secure lands and possessions in exchange for a girl's dowry. Nevertheless, love did play an important role as evidenced by the large number of clandestine or secret marriages (both in the 16th and 18th centuries) which took place without parental consent. Legislation in 1563 (the *Tametsi* clauses of the Council of Trent) and 1753 (Lord Hardwicke's Marriage Act) was to curtail the large numbers of these secret marriages with the intention of securing greater family harmony and stability (especially when marriage as contract ensured settlement of land and property).
- **Children**: It is sometimes suggested that children in the past had a brutal upbringing. Boys sent away to schools were educated through corporal punishment. There was also a custom of sending children in their teenage years as servants to relatives. The implications of this socialisation are open to considerable interpretation. But the chief motivation was to help children in the transition to the adult world (see Burguiere pp39–45).

b) Defining the family

The definition of a 'family' is just as much a philosophical one as a sociological observation. Just as 'state' might be defined as a kingdom with a monarch, or an elected government or simply the people, the notion of the family is equally problematic. As we shall see, the analogy with the state is not fortuitous for philosophers and reformers have long realised that whatever constitutes the notion of family is equally true for its larger formation as the state. Furthermore, the notion of family also defines a number of important ethical and legal issues: on inheritance, ownership, rights, sexual relationships, punishment and so on.

The notion of the family is by no means obvious. Jean-Louis Flandrin (*Families in Former Times* 1976) for instance considers what family means by surveying a number of dictionary definitions from the 17th century onwards.

- **Servants**: Some definitions (*Dictionnaire de Trevoux*, 1704–1771) distinguished between the domestic servants (including a wife) or 'domestics' of the master of a well-to-do household as his 'family' even if they lived elsewhere.
- **Co-residence/household**: Samuel Johnson (1755) defined family as 'those who live in the same house' and equivalent to the term 'household'. This included servants, as Samuel Pepys wrote in 1660, 'I lived in Axe Lane, having my wife, and servant, and no more in the family than us three'.
- **Kinship**: The significance of blood relationships has been given very different emphasis from region to region and according to historical period and class. 'The same blood', 'the same line', 'descent', 'stock', 'branch', 'parentage', 'issue' are all terms used to confirm the biological basis of family. Surprising by modern standards, blood kinship only gradually came to be the primary definition of family in the 19th century. For example, a definition of 'The Holy Family' from 1704–1752 included 'Our Lord, the Virgin, Saint Joseph and Saint John' (In the Gospel of John 19:26 Jesus says to John, his beloved disciple, that he will be a son to his mother Mary). By the late 19th century, reference to Saint John had disappeared.
- **House/lineage/class**: 'House' is used especially of the higher-ranking families. 'One says, in speaking of birth, that someone is of an honourable family and a good house, one speaks of a Royal Family, and a reigning House' (Trevoux, 1771). In other words, a family was more than simply a set of blood ties but a socially defined group. So, lower orders of society were not necessarily considered a 'family': 'Families are formed by matrimonial alliances, by polite behaviour, by conduct distinguished from that of the lower ranks, and by cultivated manners, which are passed on from father to son' (Trevoux, 1771).
- **Marriage**: By the 19th century, the two separate notions of co-residence and kinship were combined and in addition some definitions included marriage. Marriage though is a legal recognition and does not define family except from a specific ideological/class perspective.
- **Home**: The latest development in family has been the 19th century image of the 'home'. The family is the 'haven', the natural place of security, intimate relationships. It can be summed up by the Victorian adage, 'home sweet home'.

So what constitutes a family? What is the relationship and importance of the following:

- **Psychology** – sense of belonging, care, obligation, love.
- **Biology** – relationship through blood/genetics.

- **Ideology** – moral views of sexuality i.e. two parents – male and female.
- **Law** – social recognition through marriage, special rights/responsibilities.
- **Residence** – people living under the same roof or in close proximity.

c) The problem of kinship

The notion of 'kinship' which at first appears to be a simple one is affected by social custom and prevailing ideology. **Natural kinship** or **consanguinity** (legitimate or not) refers to kin related by blood or as we might now say, related genetically. In Western law today, consanguinity judges that sexual relationships between parents and grandparents and children are incestuous and illegal. **Legal affinity** applies the same prohibition of sexual relationships for adopted children, and **legitimate affinity** imposes restrictions for a married couple and the family of each of the spouses. Finally, **spiritual affinity** prohibits sexual relationships between godparents and their godchildren.

So, kinship at various times has been considered just as much in terms of spiritual and psychological bonds as it is in biological terms. The significance of these observations from the past is particularly important today. If, for instance, a family is not defined through marriage or blood relationships but the psychological ties and level of commitment of each member, then are gay and lesbian families equally legitimate? Is a family just as much a family if children are conceived using donors or brought up by step-parents?

3 The family ideal

> **KEY ISSUE**
>
> - If the family plays such an important role in the ordering of society, what is the ideal form of the family today?

Despite the observation that change to society originates first from within the family and not so much from outside, nevertheless external ideological reforms by church and state continue directly to affect the family. The family has long been regarded as the building block of society. The family constitution and organisation provide a child with his or her first experience of social existence; the values and social skills learnt in the family directly influence his or her behaviour as a member of the wider community and as a citizen. The family ideal is therefore dependent on a far more complex notion of what constitutes the ideal state. The breakdown of a particular model of the family may for some be seen as a social 'crisis' which the government should take action to remedy. Take, for instance, the following comment from the *Daily Mail* after the launch of New Labour's National Family and Parenting Institute:

> Why has Labour got it in for marriage? There could be no more telling example than the lamentably ignorant suggestion by the Home Secretary Jack Straw that marriage is not especially important in building family stability.

> D Marsland in the *Daily Mail* 2 December 1999

One of the most extreme examples of direct interference into family relationships in modern times has been in China where legislation and heavy penalties have limited married couples to one child. In Western democracies it is far from clear to what extent the state should interfere in the private relationships within a family, if by family it is understood simply the way in which people conduct their personal lives. On the other hand, if the family is considered to have a public and social role, then it might be right and proper for the state not only to make provisions for its welfare but to impose its own ideology of what constitutes a family. The tension for instance between the traditional viewpoint of the *Daily Mail* and the British government illustrates how much the notion of the family is philosophically and politically significant at the moment.

a) Classical family ideal

Cicero (106–43 BCE) said of the family:

> The origin of society is in the joining of man and woman, next in children, then in household, all things in common; this is the foundation of the city and so, to speak, the seedbed of the state.

> Cicero *On Duties* I.17.54

The classical model of a hierarchical state is reconstructed in the family. The family is essentially a little economic community (from the Greek *oikos* or house, *domus* in Latin) normally headed by the husband or **paterfamilias**. The husband thus acts as the link between the private world of the family and the public world of the state. The family is primarily defined by husband and wife and their children, but the household would include servants/slaves. In some cases slaves were allowed to marry and continued to live with their family in the household. In many ways a slave enjoyed more privileges than a freeman, though unable to own property and to take part in the state. So, as Aristotle argued in his *Politics*, compliance with the *oikonomia* or household rules (*Politics* I 1253b 1–14) was essential for the natural well-ordered family as part of society.

b) Christian family ideal

The Christian model of the family is not a fixed one. Like any other development of the family, the Christian view has been dependent on historical, economic and psychological conditions. The Bible is considered by many to be a primary source for Christian ethics, but because it was written against a range of very different cultural historical moments it does not offer one fixed ideal. This is important, for it allows modern Christian notions of the family to be flexible enough to respond to new conditions.

i Old Testament idea of the family

The Old Testament covers an immense period, but a picture of the family emerges in the first instance as a group related through birth and bound to each by kinship. Marriage was the primary means by which land and goods were transferred by treaties and alliances established between families. It should be borne in mind that the Old Testament only really describes the lives of leading families and that we know very little about ordinary families except through implication. The basic family unit was known as the *bet av*, or simply *bait* 'the house', and like the classical model was a paterfamilias. The *bait* might also refer to the extended family and sometimes in that context was known as *mishpachah* (i.e. all those related to each other living and dead). The *mishpachah* ensured that land remained within the family by encouraging marriages within the extended family. It is for this reason that there were such detailed prohibitions of incest (Leviticus 18:7–18) and we can see the need to ensure tight control of personal relationships in close and complex families.

- **Polygamy or monogamy?** King David had seven wives (1 Chronicles 3:1–9) and King Solomon seven hundred as well as three hundred concubines (1 Kings 11:3). However, by the time of the Second Temple period (586 BCE onwards) the implication was that monogamy had become the norm – the book of Tobit (c 200 BCE) assumes monogamy.
- **Family life** The patriarchal narratives vividly portray some of the tensions of a family living in close proximity. Abraham, the paterfamilias and his brother's son Lot agree to split the family (*bet av*) after squabbling among their herdsmen and Lot settles in the fertile land of the Jordan valley (Genesis 13). Cain kills his brother Abel (Genesis 4) and Jacob, encouraged by his scheming mother, Rebekah, tricks his father Isaac to give him his brother Esau's birthright (Genesis 27). Later David's son Amnon rapes his half sister Tamar and then is murdered on the instruction of Tamar's brother Absolom (2 Samuel 13).
- **Social model**: The intrigues of family serve in theological terms to illustrate that despite human frailty the family is nevertheless the source of social behaviour. Job describes it as the haven (Job 19) and the law allowed a family to seek blood vengeance on the murderer of any of

their kinsmen. Families who fell on hard times were to be supported by the wider family; the brother-in-law of a childless widow had a duty to enable her to have a child.

● **Law** The law or Torah and later the prophets frequently legislate to protect the family against the exploitation of richer and more powerful men. In order to survive the famines which frequently devastated Israel, men and women sold themselves into slavery and lands and essential goods were exchanged for food. But the Torah ensures that these must only be temporary arrangements – slaves must be freed and women slaves elevated to wives (Exodus 21:2–11), loans must be interest free (Exodus 22:25–27), the family must be preserved.

But the most important feature of the family ideal is what John Rogerson calls the 'structure of grace' (*The Family in Theological Perspective* pp 36–41). It is a theological ideal which originates in the experience of the family and only then becomes embodied into the Torah in what is known as the **Book of Covenant** (Exodus 21:1-23:19). It is the family experience of God's love and concern for the family, his willingness to forgive as well as protect. It is the source of justice for all regardless of social status and gender. Yet despite the ideal, it needed the imagination of the writer of Deuteronomy (7th Century BCE) and the poetic inspiration of the prophets for the people of Israel to live up to their special understanding of the family ideal. But it is the vision of Deuteronomy which transforms the family ideal into a nationwide social means of justice. In language which is later to become characteristic of monasteries and communist states, Deuteronomy extends the use of 'brother' to all members of society – including one's enemies:

1 If there is among you a poor man, one of your brethren, in any of your towns within your land which the Lord your God gives you, you shall not harden your heart or shut your hand against your poor brother but you shall open your hand to him, and lend him sufficient for his need,
5 whatever it may be.

Deuteronomy 15:7–8

Much later after the restoration of Israel (*c* 530 BCE) Nehemiah issued several edicts to the reconstituted community (Nehemiah 5:2–5) based on the Deuteronomic family ethic of grace. In other words the family ideal was not just an abstract idea.

ii The New Testament idea of the family

The New Testament has an ambivalent view of the family. The Gospels, on the one hand, suggest that Jesus placed the obligations of the Kingdom of God before family duties (Mark 3:31–35, Matthew 8:21–22, Luke 14:26):

1 And his mother and his brothers came; and standing outside they sent
to him and called him. And a crowd was sitting about him; and they said
to him, 'Your mother and your brothers are outside, asking for you.' And
he replied, 'Who are my mother and my brothers?' And looking around
5 on those who sat about him, he said, 'Here are my mother and my
brothers! Whoever does the will of God is my brother, and sister, and
mother.'

Mark 3:31–35

On the other hand, Jesus' teaching on the permanency of marriage
as a symbol of the original covenant established between God and his
creation suggests that the family is a particularly important expression
of the Kingdom of God on earth (see page 101 for a more detailed
discussion).

The same ambivalence is also to be found in the writings of St Paul.
Paul appears to elevate the celibate life above the married state (1
Corinthians 7:8, 38) whilst also reiterating the teaching of Jesus on
life-long monogamous marriage (1 Corinthians 7:2–4). But by second
and third generation Christianity the idea of the family is most clearly
expressed in what Luther called the *Haustafelen* or household rules
(Ephesians 5:22–6:9, 1 Peter 2:18–3:7, 1 Timothy 2:8–15, 6:1–2, Titus
2:1–10). For example:

1 Wives, be subject to your husbands, as is fitting in the Lord. Husbands,
love your wives, and do not be harsh with them. Children, obey your
parents in everything, for this pleases the Lord. Fathers, do not provoke
your children, lest they become discouraged. Slaves, obey in everything
5 those who are your earthly masters, not with eyeservice, as men-
pleasers, but in singleness of heart, fearing the Lord. Whatever your
task, work heartily, as serving the Lord and not men, knowing that from
the Lord you will receive the inheritance as your reward; you are
serving the Lord Christ. For the wrongdoer will be paid back for the
10 wrong he has done, and there is no partiality. Masters, treat your slaves
justly and fairly, knowing that you also have a Master in heaven.

Colossians 3:18–4:1

All these lists developed from the idea of presenting Christianity in a
socially acceptable form to the world in which it was evolving. The
pattern of these rules reflect the typical patriarchal paterfamilias of
the time (including slaves which even the humblest of families would
have had). James Dunn (in S Barton *The Family in Theological
Perspective* p49f) argues that the widespread existence of household
rules from the Greek political and philosophical world provided a
framework within which the early Christians could operate. The
characteristic of the Colossians passage is that:

● It addresses to each tier of the family as equals (male, female, child and
slave).

- The frequent references to the 'Lord' suggest that the rules are considered to be a Christian duty and that the list is not simply borrowed wholesale from a Greek or Jewish source (J Dunn *The Family* p52).
- The list probably has its own origins in Jesus' own reinforcement of the fifth commandment (Exodus 20:12) to honour mother and father (Mark 10:19) and his frequent use of children as examples of true discipleship (Mark 10:13–16).
- The lists therefore amplified the earlier teaching of Paul that even though becoming a member of the 'family' of Christ (Romans 8:16-17, 29) meant to enter a relationship of friendship ('brotherhood') between men and women, free and slave (Galatians 3:27–28) this did not preclude specific duties and responsibilities.
- The lists also provided, by analogy, orderliness and duties for house churches as an expression of the church as the 'family' of Christ (see 1 Timothy 3:2–5). So, despite the Christian ideal of equality, the prohibition of women taking an instructional role in church gatherings resulted from the desire of the early writers to present Christianity as a way of life which would not threaten the wider social order but would work within it.

iii Christian traditional view of the family

The church in all its various traditions has from early times distinguished between two kinds of love. Christian love or *agape* is the love of Christ and independent from human or natural love. As we have seen from the writings of St Paul, the single life is often preferred to family life for this reason. Paul's views were often exaggerated in strong terms by later Christian theologians. For example St Jerome (*c* 342–420 CE) writes:

1   He who is too ardently amorous of his wife is also an adulterer. With regard to the wife of another, in truth, all love is disgraceful; and with regard to one's own wife, excessive love is. The wise man must love his wife with judgement, not passion. Let him curb his transports of
5   voluptuousness and not let himself be urged precipitately to indulge in coition. Nothing is more vile than to love a wife like a mistress.

Jerome *Against Jovinian* I.49

Selfish love has long been associated with **concupiscence**, the rebellious side of human nature resulting from original sin. Selfish love is manifested in many other ways: in the lax bringing up of children, marrying children to pay off debts through a dowry. Discipline and control of concupiscence underlined the commandment for children to be obedient to their parents' wishes. One of the reasons that the *tametsi* clause of the Council of Trent (1563) prohibited clandestine marriage was in order to reinforce the control of parents over their children and at the same time satisfy the household rules set out in the New Testament.

Thomas Aquinas (*c*1225–1274) following the Western tradition of **St Augustine** (354–430) argued from natural law that children's education was a primary duty of parents. For just as God sustains the creation spiritually and physically so it follows that parents have a duty to their children to feed and educate them personally. Thus the emergent Christian ideology differed from the classical model where the state undertook the education of children. This is now firmly established in the modern Christian Church, as this passage from the most recent Catholic catechism illustrates:

1   The fecundity of conjugal love cannot be reduced solely to the procreation of children, but must extend to their moral education and their spiritual formation. 'The role of parents in education is of such importance that it is almost to provide an adequate substitute.' The
5   right and duty of parents to educate their children are primordial and inalienable. Parents must regard their children as children of God and respect them as human persons. Showing themselves obedient to the will of the Father in heaven, they educate their children to fulfil God's law... By knowing how to acknowledge their own failings to their
10 children, parents will be better able to guide and correct them:

'He who loves his son will not spare the rod... He who disciplines his son will profit by him.' (Sirach 30:1–2)

Catechism of the Catholic Church (1994) pp 479–480

There is no doubt that sin and sex posed a problem for many of the early theologians. But as Carol Harrison (in S Barton *The Family in Theological Perspective* pages 92–97) argues, the Church Fathers were not unaware that the vast majority of Christians were married and lived in families. Augustine used the classical family model in his *City of God* (chapter 19) and like Cicero considered the family to be the natural God-given building block of society. The theological problems of the transmission of sin through sex could be avoided when considering that Adam and Eve had been created by God for each other without sexual generation, as a family, based on friendship and mutual companionship (*concordia*, i.e. 'with the heart'). The view is developed especially in his depiction of Mary and Joseph and the holy family to illustrate the importance of the family into which Christ was born (*Against Faustus* 23.8). The family can express affectionate love. Augustine wrote that a wife is:

One's partner for life...should never be fettered with fear and threats, but with love and patience... what sort of satisfaction could a husband himself have, if he lives with his wife as if she were a slave, and not with a woman by her own free will.

Augustine *Homily 20 on Ephesians* 5:22–33

Theologians today do not often make such sharp distinction between erotic and affectionate love. Sex which is pleasurable is not regarded as the transmission of sin, providing both partners love and treat each other as people and not as objects. Pre-marital sex (sex before marriage) is generally considered to be detrimental to the formation of stable, long-term and loving families because it lacks the life-long commitment of husband and wife which is essential to the Christian family ideal. A movement in America called **The Promise Keepers** (its members pledge only to have sex within marriage) is an example of those who feel that the family ideal is being eroded through promiscuous sexual behaviour. Some of the criticisms of modern Western societies made by Christian theologians include:

● Christian ideology is concerned by the eroticisation of Western society. Love as pleasure has preceded love as commitment.
● Christian ideology considers that couples are often too private and egocentric in their relationships (whereas the Christian family should be outward looking to the wider community).
● Couples expect too much from their relationship often exacerbated by unobtainable images in the media. Traditional Christian ideology teaches that mutual affection is the basis for secure families.
● Essential social values learnt in the home are being destroyed through the disintegration of the family.

Finally, the Church has used the image of the family to describe various other institutions. The Church has often likened the family to a 'domestic Church' (through education, order, discipline, prayer, baptism, marriage), but equally monastic institutions and even the church itself have been described in family terms. The Church is the 'bride of Christ' and the Virgin Mary, Christ's wife. Those who enter the monastic life are wedded to Christ and its life is seen in communal family terms. Ambivalence about the family in favour of the single life if anything is reversed:

> Some forgo marriage in order to care for their parents or brothers and sisters, to give themselves more completely to a profession, or to serve other honourable ends. They can contribute greatly to the good of the human family.
>
> *Catechism of the Catholic Church* (1994) p481

iv Criticisms of the Christian family ideology

● It has historically lacked a social perspective. It has never obliged families to redistribute wealth for instance.
● It has never helped members of society escape their social position (e.g. Islam enables women to avoid poverty through polygamy).

- Christian ideology has not, until recent times, allowed for couples to regulate the size of their families (contraception is still prohibited by the Roman Catholic Church, and abortion is generally considered to be morally unacceptable).
- Family roles are dominated by a patriarchal structure, which is hierarchical (either by placing the husband as 'head of the wife' or by making children subservient to their parents).
- It makes too stringent and unrealistic demands on parents and children
- It has a repressed and confused teaching on human sexuality, especially when considered as the transmission of sin.

c) Alternative family ideals

Throughout the modern period there have been many attempts to set up rival family models. At one extreme there are those who reject the very idea of family, whilst others look to radical reform. Is it possible to say what a 'proper' family is?

i Communitarian

There have been many experiments, religious and secular in the radical reordering of the family as a community. Communitarian ideologies have shared the common view that humans are essentially good and, in the right conditions, will live in peace and harmony. Some, such as Leo Tolstoy (1828–1910), established his 'farms' motivated by the desire to set up model communities as the means of prompting wider social reforms. Tolstoy was impressed by Jesus' Sermon on the Mount (Matthew 5–7) and inspired by the transforming effect Jesus' teaching had on the early Christians:

> And all who believed were together and had all things in common; and they sold their possessions and goods and distributed them to all, as any had need.
>
> Acts of the Apostles 2:44–45

But the most radical alternatives, often based on Marxist ideology, have argued that true community can only be established if the notion of the self-contained family is abolished. Thus if the education and rearing of children, work and employment are all centralised and controlled by the community itself, then competition between families, the acquisition of wealth and status will all fade away leaving people to form their relationships freely. Taboos on sexual unions (so often based on religious superstition), as this passage from Frederick Engels illustrates, would also be abolished:

> With the transfer of the means of production into common ownership, the single family ceases to be the economic unit of society. Private housekeeping is transformed into a social industry. The care and education of the children becomes a public affair; society looks

5   after all children alike, whether they are legitimate or not. This removes all anxiety about the 'consequences', which today is the most essential social – moral as well as economic – factor that prevents a girl giving herself completely to the man she loves. Will not that suffice to bring about the gradual growth of unconstrained sexual intercourse and

10 with it a more tolerant public opinion in regard to a maiden's honour and a woman's shame?

F Engels *The Origin of the Family, Private Property and the State* (1884) p107

Marxism has been variously interpreted, and much like the growth of Christianity, its establishment and formation has varied enormously. Engels' essay has often been criticised for its lack of trustworthy anthropological evidence to support his developmental view of the family through its various historical stages (to its final and liberated form). The implementation of Marxist ideology in Russia (and the former USSR) has led some to criticise it on the following grounds (see Burguiere et al. *A History of the Family* Volume 2 Chapter 11):

- **Independence** Families have wanted independence and a sense of their own worth and identity through ownership of property. In 1935, the Russian government passed the *Kolkhoz* law guaranteeing the private ownership of property.
- **Love** The Marxist model concentrates almost entirely on the liberation of individuals from economic exploitation and ownership. But liberation is not enough, and Engels' libertarian encouragement of open sex takes little account of the jealousy and hurt this can cause. In Russia pressure from the peasants in the 1920s forced the government to reintroduce laws to protect the family.
- **Children** Engels' model concentrated almost entirely on the abolition of marriage and little account is taken of the natural desire of parents to nurture their own children. Liberal divorce arrangements and strong intervention of the state into children's education has led to large numbers of dysfunctional children.
- **Environment** The socialist model has tested the proposition that a change of environment (crèches, education, work practices) is sufficient to change behaviour and social attitudes. Russian women complain that men continue to discriminate against them both in the work place and at home.

ii Feminist family networks

As Chapter 3 makes clear, there is no one feminist viewpoint. However, for many feminists the traditional nuclear family not only perpetuates outmoded gender roles, but even when the woman has her own economic freedom (outside the home), it can exploit her in other ways. There is a great deal of discussion as to whether a woman can balance a job and family. Germaine Greer (*Sex and Destiny* 1984) argues that the nuclear family places far too many economic and psychological burdens on each member of the family. The nuclear family has become increasingly isolated, making relationships too intense and expectations too high. But above all the woman has lacked the support from other women, which she would have had in the extended family. Greer is impressed by the way in which extended families work outside the European model (in India for instance):

1   It may seem strange for a twentieth-century feminist to be among the few champions of the Family as a larger organisation than the suburban dyad, for most Families are headed by men and men play the decisive roles in them, or at any rate usually appear to, but there are reasons

5   for such a paradoxical attitude. For one thing, if the family is to be a female sphere, then it is better for women's sanity and tranquillity that they not be isolated in it, as they are in the nuclear family. The Family offers the paradigm for the female collectivity; it shows us women co-operating to dignify their lives, to lighten each other's labour, and

10 growing in real love and sisterhood, a word we use constantly without any idea of what it is... Women in the extended family are not at the mercy of their husbands; indeed their relationship with their husband's mother, may well be more important... Women in the extended Family are not an object but an agent; the Family's prosperity and

15 cohesiveness will be directly due to her. She does not briefly blaze as her husband's paramour and decline into the whining mother of one or two, until she becomes that most loathed of Western species, a mother-in-law *cum* blue-rinsed widow; she has the opportunity to develop and to play an increasingly important role for an increasing

20 number of people, until infirmity deposes her.

G Greer Sex and Destiny (1984) pp241–244

The importance of the feminist ideology is that it looks beyond the immediate bounds of the nuclear family and stresses its wider links as part of a web of relationships free from the hierarchical and self-contained view of the patriarchal nuclear family. Secondly, the feminist ideology has rediscovered what is often observed in other cultures, that the centrality of the conjugal bond (i.e. of mother and father) is less important than the significance of other relationships within the wider family (aunts, cousins, grandparents and so on). Thirdly, feminism has enabled Christian families to revive important Christian virtues of forgiveness, co-operation, care and shared responsibilities.

Criticisms of feminist families include:

● Radical feminism considers the heterosexual family to be fundamentally flawed; it will never allow women to find equality and freedom from sexist stereotyping.

● Many feminists are deeply critical of liberal feminists (see pages xx) who, by stressing individual women's rights, fail to see the family in holistic and communitarian terms.

● Feminism can set up false hopes for women and cause gender confusion and instability in the family.

iii Gay and lesbian model: friends as family

The most recent trend in family ideology has emerged from gay and lesbian relationships. Family has come to refer to a circle of chosen and close gay friends independent from a family based on consanguinity. The key notion is the sense of 'belonging to' and commitment to others. Jeffrey Weeks *et al.* (*The New Family?* 1999) cite the following quotation from a black lesbian as typical of many:

> I think the friendships I have are family. I'm sure lots of people will say this, but, it's very important to me because my family are not – apart from my mother, who's kind of important – on the whole my family's all I've got. And my family are my friends. And I think you make your family – because I've never felt like I belonged anywhere.
>
> J Weeks in E Silva and C Smart *The New Family?* (1999) p87

So, friendship has been transformed into a kinship relationship, which, in the language of philosophers and sociologists, has its own narrative. In other words, gay and lesbian people feel a powerful common identity because of their shared sexuality and also a subjective narrative which is self-defined, chosen and creative (see how the philosopher Foucault considers this notion on page 10), independent from objective blood kinship ties within traditional heterosexual families. The result is an important family paradigm shift. The homosexual family is an active process of 'doing', whereas for heterosexuals it is more a passive state of 'being'. Perhaps with an increased knowledge of homosexuality and more fluid relationships, the friendship model of family is beginning to be adopted by many heterosexuals as well, blurring the sense of obligation to blood family and friends.

> The distinctiveness that they find in same-sex households may increasingly be shared by newly emergent patterns in heterosexual relationships where commitment may be a matter of negotiation, rather than ascription.
>
> E Silva and C Smart *The New Family?* (1999) p8

4 Some issues for the family today

KEY ISSUE

● What are the legal and moral issues which face children and parents in a time of social change?

Whatever the ideology of the family none is free from its own particular moral and social dilemmas. Set out below are a few of the issues which families are having to face today. Each should be considered against the various family ideals discussed so far.

a) Fatherhood and motherhood after divorce

In order to remedy some of the psychological damage done to children after divorce, the debates of the 1980s onwards have shifted post-divorce legal arrangements away from purely financial commitments to providing shared parental care and responsibility. In England and Wales this new thinking resulted in the 1989 Children Act. The main implications are that:

● Parental relationships to children remain the same after as before divorce.
● There are now no orders for 'custody', instead the courts make orders for 'residency' and 'contact' (previously called 'access').
● Parents are encouraged to make their own private arrangements (whereas previously the courts set out 'orders').

As Carol Smart observes (Silva and Smart *The New Family?* Chapter 3), this opens up a new range of possibilities not only for the notion of fatherhood but also motherhood. Clearly the conditions are quite different from when the couple shared a common emotional and economic situation. Smart suggests that this 'might start the gradual transformation of both motherhood and fatherhood at the end of the twentieth century'. But is this desirable? Smart's analysis revealed:

● How reluctant men were at taking on equal responsibility of the children with their former wife or partner.
● Most men were willing to let their former partner take the brunt of responsibility, although many objected to being told how to look after the children and felt constrained that the women controlled the new relationship.
● Men who adjusted found their roles as fathers to be far more active than when they were married, but many women found this very hard to accommodate with their in-built sense of motherhood.

Smart concludes that it is women who appear to lose out. The solution is for mothers to 'behave more like fathers during marriage in order to ameliorate the future deficit to their status as citizens in the context of a modern welfare state which increasingly values paid work' (p113). In other words, the notion that parents can effectively operate for the benefit of their children after divorce or separation depends on whether men and women really can (or should) alter their gender expectations.

There is also the complication of step-parents and new partners and their relationship with the genetic parents. Whilst some argue positively for enriching experience that a child might gain by having a new range of kinship group arrangements (and consider how normal such families were in the past see page 158), others consider that this is really a self-centred adult excuse for personal freedom.

b) Gender roles

The impact of feminism has posed particular challenges to the functioning of the family. The challenge of certain forms of feminism has been a source of liberation for both sexes. Lack of traditional gender roles has freed couples to create their own particular relationship – a man may choose the 'private' role as the one who rears the children whilst the woman pursues the 'public' role as bread-winner: the essence is to achieve existential and spiritual fulfilment. But paradoxically whilst men and women are freer to form more stable satisfactory relationships observers have noted that increasing individualism has made it harder for couples to know what to expect from each other.

i Employment

In practice the shift in gender expectations has simply added to the complexity of family roles. Men may feel that it is their role to provide an income for the family whilst it is still the woman's role to manage the household chores even if she also is a wage earner.

● Increased employment and earning power of women, its importance for self-esteem as well as economic independence has made marriage and the family increasingly more contingent and less important.
● Employers are yet to give men the same flexible working arrangements as women (paternity leave, prejudice against a man leaving work to mind the family).

ii Household roles

What roles should modern men and women play today? From the woman's perspective so much will depend on her particular experience of feminism. Some such as Jean Bethke Elshtain consider that women have a special role to play as carers in the home in the rearing of children; whilst for others, such as Shulamith Firestone (see page 29), the rearing and nurturing of children is quite independent from being a women (modern reproductive technologies have now made this possible) a woman's self worth in production (work) is not to be equated with reproduction (child rearing). The issue may appear trivial as to who is responsible for the household chores (washing, cooking, cleaning, ironing, etc.) but at stake is the question of identity, self worth and a sense of fairness. The result of such conflicting views can be the cause of great tension between all members of the family.

- Sociologists note that in British society at least gender inequality is more pronounced at home than in the work place. Very many men at least have traditional expectations of women's duties – this is reflected to a large extent in the way advertisements are aimed at the woman for home commodities and appliances.
- Because the majority of women are in low paid, part time jobs the impact of economic independence is less than might be expected,
- Research has indicated that in gay and lesbian relationships fairness is more often achieved by division of tasks because couples are free from traditional heterosexual gendered expectations of duty (Elizabeth Silva in Silva and Smart *The New Family?* p48).

c) Homosexual adoption of children

Should a gay or lesbian couple have the right to adopt a child and be considered a family in line with a heterosexual couple? In a landmark ruling (*Fitzpatrick* v. *Stirling Housing*, 2 November 1999) the House of Lords judged that a homosexual couple in stable relationship could be considered a family. The reason in this case was to enable a gay partner the right to inherit his or her partner's tenancy. The significance of the ruling is that it understood 'family' in terms of a couple living in the same household. So, if for the purposes of inheritance a gay couple can be considered a family, the question is whether family rights should also be extended to the adoption of a child.

i Quality of relationship

Under existing English law (1976 Adoption Act) an unmarried individual may adopt. If it is accepted that a single woman would make a good adoptive parent for a child with special needs (as the 1993 Conservative Government's white paper *Adoption; the Future* argued), then the principle seems to be that parenthood is more to do with the quality of relationship (i.e. stability, love, long-term care) than gender specific requirements. This will be hard to assess. There will be those who argue that homosexual relationships tend to be short-term, unhealthy and a perversion of moral norms (see Chapter 4), but then some heterosexual cohabitation relationships might also be considered to be prone to be short-term and morally unacceptable. Furthermore, does it necessarily follow that if a heterosexual couple are married then their relationship will make them better parents?

ii Rights

Some argue that a homosexual couple should be able to adopt a child based on human rights. For a woman in a lesbian relationship any baby she may conceive is entirely her legal responsibility if she chooses not to reveal the father (or she conceives through an anonymous donor sperm). For a man it is less straightforward, unless the surrogate mother specifically nominates the father. The question in each case is whether the law should acknowledge the right of the homosexual partner as a full legal adoptive parent. Equally, the law will have to decide whether a child is entitled to two parents regardless of gender, or a mother and a father. The 1989 Children Act allows a joint residence order for the non-adopting partner (sometimes referred to as the 'co-parent') to have some responsibility over the child, but this offers no guarantee, if a partnership should dissolve, that the non-adopting partner would have right of access to the child.

In California, however, where there is a large gay community, Proposition 22 was rejected in March 2000. The proposition would have allowed gay men to marry but as one campaigner said, 'It's a victory for California families. We think this will send a strong message to our children for the future of the institution of marriage – that it should remain between a man and woman' (*The Times* 9 March 2000)

d) Children: care, abuse and incest

How much autonomy should a family have to run and discipline its children in its own way? Over the past hundred years divorce laws have increasingly given more protection and independence to women from their husbands. Now over the past decade attention has turned to the independence and protection of children against abuse from their parents. This raises some fundamental questions about the degree of independence parents have to discipline their children as they wish and the kind of relationships which they are allowed to form within the limits of acceptability imposed by the wider community. Has the state the right to break up a family and remove children from what it considers to be abusive parents?

i What is abuse?

The notion of abuse is inevitably subjective and fluid. There is, for instance, considerable debate whether a parent who uses corporal punishment to discipline a child is blameworthy of 'abuse'. Many commentators consider that the idea of 'child abuse' has arisen from the feminisation of society and an emphasis on the interior experience of children. Abuse is, therefore, any form of power over a child, with or without consent, to their psychological detriment. Abuse destroys the responsibility of the role of the carer by treating the child as a means to self-gratification and as an object rather than a person in their own right.

ii Parental roles

Abuse in this context challenges traditional parental roles and the autonomy of the family. There are more subtle challenges though. Does it necessarily follow that the traditional patriarchal family is more likely to lead to the abuse of children by the father? Evidence suggests that the traditional role of the woman as 'carer' obscures the fact that many women are directly or indirectly (by turning a blind eye) involved in child sexual abuse.

iii Empowerment

How can children be protected from abuse? There is no simple answer. Schools have a role in educating the young to be aware that certain forms of sexual relationships are wrong. But how can this be done without frightening and alienating children from their parents? Better still is the education of adults and especially women to act as role models to their children. Seeing a mother resist an abusive father, it is argued, empowers children to do the same. There are implications also for caring institutions (churches, schools, and children's homes) and growing awareness that they can also be the cause of abuse as well as the means for helping abused families.

iv Incest and sexual abuse

Is **incest** necessarily to be equated with sex abuse? The extremely fine line between sensuous and sexual love in the family is imaginatively related in Ian McEwan's novel *The Cement Garden* (1980). Following the death of their parents brother and sister find themselves over the summer holidays forming a closer and closer sexual relationship. The story ends when the police enter the house and find the two having sexual intercourse. On one level the intimacy of their relationship does not suggest that what they have done is perverted or disgusting. Those who look for the abolition of incest laws do so on the grounds that many of these ancient taboos relate to very different cultures and periods of history and that on rational utilitarian grounds providing all parties are happy there can be no harm in it. But the significance of the McEwan's story is that the relationship has only formed in this way because the family has collapsed. Incest is therefore sexual abuse of children because it denies the intimacy of parents as carers of their children. Perhaps there is a similar analogy at the adult level with adultery: for adultery replaces friendship (however intimate) outside marriage by destroying the special relationship of trust and intimacy between husband and wife.

v Parental responsibility of young adults

At what stage do parents relinquish their disciplinary and caring role? All parents know that childhood is a fluid term; some children grow up quicker than others. Parental care might be said never to end but more complex is knowing at what stage parents have to adapt and relinquish their disciplinary roles. For instance, British law in 1885 raised the age of consent from 13 to 16 but lowered the age of majority from 21 to 18 in 1969 (Family Reform Act). The law sends out conflicting signals to parents. An illustration of parental dilemmas is in the important legal case of Mrs Victoria Gillick (*Gillick v. West Norfolk Health Authority* 1986).

Mrs Gillick challenged the local health authority's policy of allowing medical practitioners to give contraceptive advice and treatment to children below the age of 16 without parental consent and knowledge. The complexity of the case meant that it eventually went to the House of Lords. In the first instance the Lords favoured Mrs Gillick's contention that parents should be consulted. But a few months later the decision was overturned in favour of Lord Scarman's **test of competence** that a child is legally competent to consent to medical treatment when he or she 'achieves a sufficient understanding and intelligence to enable him or her to understand fully what is proposed'. However, it is Lord Scarman's further comment which has had much wider implications for parent-child responsibility:

> Parental rights... do not wholly disappear until the age of majority...But the common law has never treated such rights as sovereign or beyond review and control. Nor has our law ever treated the child as other than a person with capacities and rights recognised by law. The principle of the law... is that parental rights are derived from parental duty and exist only so long as they are needed for the protection of the person and property of the child.

Gillick v. West Norfolk and Wisbech AHA [1986] AC 183–184

According to Department of Health statistics, in 1996–1997 there were 102,000 under-age girls who were prescribed contraception (i.e. over one in ten under-age girls). Does this indicate that parents simply don't care about their children or has society made it very difficult for them to exert any authority? What are the implications for the ancient idea that the household should be the place of order (see household rules above)? The frequent utilitarian response of the health authorities (and many parents) is that it is better to give children contraception than no contraception but yet again many like Mrs Gillick doubt the effectiveness of utilitarianism as the basis of a social ethic.

Answering structured and essay questions

Summary diagram

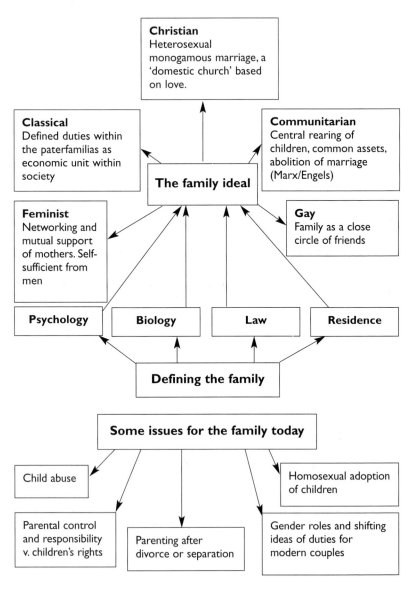

Questions

1. **a)** Describe the main characteristics of the family as presented in the Bible.
    b) Assess the view that the Christian family is sexist and patriarchal.

2. **a)** Explain the reasons why many consider the family to be on the decline.
    b) How far have women's movements been responsible for family problems?

3. Discuss whether parents should be given more or less power over their children?

4. 'The nuclear family is the source of all that is wrong in society' Discuss.

5. Assess the view that gay or lesbian couples should be allowed to adopt children and be considered a family.

Essay skills

Essays on the family require some historical knowledge and basic sociology. Factual or empirical knowledge is particularly difficult to pin down and you must make sure you use the data as part of an argument. Words such as 'decline' presuppose that there was something better before hand. 'Patriarchal' is a feminist criticism and assumes that alternatives are wrong. 'Power over' is deliberately biased and hints at the idea of 'abuse' rather than 'discipline'. The philosophical arguments must flow from a more general picture of what society should be like; so issues of gender, freedom/autonomy, sexual lifestyle, law and morality need to be defined carefully. Other chapters in this book should be consulted if necessary.

Further reading

D. Alton *Life after Death* Christian Democratic Press 1999

M. Banner *Christian Ethics and Contemporary Moral Problems* CUP 1999

S. Barton (editor) *The Family in Theological Perspective* T and T Clarke 1996

J. Baycroft (editor) *Whose Child is This?* Anglican Book Centre, Toronto 1990

J. Bentham *An Introduction to the Principles of Morals and Legislation* in M. Warnock (editor) *Utilitarianism* Fount 1962

M. Blasius and S. Phelan (editors) *We are Everywhere: A Historical Sourcebook of Gay and Lesbian Politics* Routledge 1997

Board for Social Responsibility *Personal Origins* Church House Publishing, second revised edition 1996

British Medical Association *The Changing Conception of Motherhood* British Medical Association 1996

D. Brown *Choices: Ethics and the Christian* Blackwell 1983

P. Brown *The Body and Society* Faber and Faber 1990

A. Burguiere, C. Klapisch-Zuber, M Segalen and F Zonabend *A History of the Family* Volume II Polity Press 1996

L. Cahill *Sex, Gender and Christian Ethics* Cambridge University Press 1996

Catechism of the Catholic Church English translation Chapman 1994

Catholic Truth Society *Declaration on Certain Questions Concerning Sexual Ethics*

The Code of Canon Law English translation Collins 1983

J. Collingwood *Common Law Marriage* Grove 1994

L W Countryman *Dirt, Greed and Sex* SCM/X Press reprints, 1989/1996

J. Dominion *Marriage, Faith and Love* Fount 1981

J. Dominion and H. Montefiore *God, Sex and Love* SCM 1989

C. Donnellan (editor) *Surrogacy and IVF* Independence Educational Publishers 1997

C. Donnellan (editor) *Homosexuality* Independence 1998

C. Donnellan (editor) *Separation and Divorce* Independence 1999

A. Dyson *The Ethics of IVF* Mowbray 1995

F. Engels *The Origin of the Family, Private Property, and the State* edited I. Barratt, Penguin 1986

D. Flanagan and T. Williams *Cohabitation or Marriage?* CARE 1997

J-L. Flandrin *Families in Former Times* translated by R. Southern, Cambridge University Press 1979

R. Fletcher *The Shaking of the Foundations: Family and Society* Routledge 1988

M. Foucault *The History of Sexuality: the Will to Knowledge* (1976) translated by R Hurley, Penguin 1979

R. Gill *A Texbook of Christian Ethics* T and T Clark, second edition, 1995

G. Greer *Sex and Destiny* Secker and Warburg 1984

D. Hampson *After Christianity* SCM 1996

A. Harvey *Strenuous Commands* SCM/X Press Reprints 1990/1996
T. Hitchcock *English Sexualities 1700–1800* Macmillian Press 1997
R. Holloway (editor) *Who Needs Feminism?* SPCK 1991
Issues in Human Sexuality: A Statement by the House of Bishops Church House Publishing 1991
G. Jenkins *Cohabitation: A Biblical Perspective* Grove, 1992
J. Jeremias *Jerusalem in the time of Jesus* SCM, 1969, 1973
R. Jones *Groundwork of Christian Ethics* Epworth 1984
K. Kelly *New Directions in Sexual Ethics* Cassell 1998
A. Loades (editor) *Feminist Theology: A Reader* SPCK 1991
C. Molloy *Marriage: Theology and Reality* Columbia Press/Novalis 1996
New Dictionary of Theology, The Gill and Macmillan 1990
R. Nicolson *God in Aids?* SCM 1996
R. Nye (editor) *Sexuality* Oxford University Press, 1999
A. Oakley *Sex, Gender and Society* Arena 1972, 1985
A. Oakley *Woman's Work: The Housewife, Past and Present* Pantheon Books 1974
H. Oppenheimer *Marriage* Mowbrays 1990
S. Parsons *Feminism and Christian Ethics* Cambridge University Press 1996
G. Pence *Classic Cases In Medical Ethics* McGraw-Hill, 1995
Personal Origins second revised edition, Church House Publishing, 1996
R. Phillips *Untying the Knot* Cambridge University Press 1991
E. Pratt *Living in Sin?* St Simon's Church 1994
K. Rudy *Sex and the Church* Beacon Press 1997
R. Ruether *Sexism and God-Talk* SCM 1983
B. Russell *Marriage and Morals* George Unwin 1929
T. Schmidt *Straight and Narrow?* Inter Varsity Press 1995
E. Silva and C. Smart (editors) *The New Family?* Sage Publications 1999
P. Singer *A Companion to Ethics* Blackwell 1991
Social Trends 29 Office for National Statistics, Stationery Office 1999
Something to Celebrate: Valuing Families in Church and Society Church House Publishing 1995
T. Spargo *Foucault and Queer Theory* Icon Books 1999
P. Taylor *For Better or for Worse* CARE 1998
H. Thielicke *The Ethics of Sex* James Clarke 1964
M. Thompson *Ethical Theory* Hodder and Stoughton 1999
R. Tong *Feminist Thought: a Comprehensive Introduction* Routledge 1992
P. Vardy *The Puzzle of Sex* Fount 1997
M. Wilcockson *Issues of Life and Death* Hodder and Stoughton 1999
A. Winnett *The Church and Divorce* Mowbrays 1968

Index